"Why did you have to get a divorce? And when can I get a hamster?"

ALSO BY ANTHONY E. WOLF

"Get out of my life, but first could you drive me and Cheryl to the mall?" A Parent's Guide to the New Teenager

"It's not fair, Jeremy Spencer's parents let him stay up all night!" A Guide to the Tougher Parts of Parenting

Anthony E. Wolf, Ph.D.

ILLUSTRATIONS BY THE AUTHOR

THE NOONDAY PRESS
FARRAR, STRAUS AND GIROUX
NEW YORK

"Why did you have to get a divorce? And when can I get a hamster?"

A GUIDE TO PARENTING
THROUGH DIVORCE

The Noonday Press
A division of Farrar, Straus and Giroux
19 Union Square West, New York 10003

Distributed in Canada by Douglas & McIntyre Ltd.
Printed in the United States of America
Designed by Peter Buchanan-Smith
First edition, 1998
Second printing, 1998
Library of Congress Cataloging-in-Publication Data
Wolf, Anthony E.
"Why did you have to get a divorce? And when can I get a
hamster?" : a guide to parenting through divorce / Anthony E. Wolf.
  p.   cm.
ISBN 0-374-52568-4 (alk. paper)
  1. Children of divorced parents — Psychology.   2. Parenting.
3. Divorced parents — Psychology.   4. Divorce — Psychological aspects.
I. Title.
HQ777.5.W65   1998
649'.1 — dc21   98-14895

To Mary Alice, Nick, and Margaret

Acknowledgments

This book was edited by Patty Bryan. I am continually grateful for her skill, patience, and wisdom in helping put together this and my two previous books. I would also like to thank Mike Bryan for his help in the editing of this book.

I want to thank Billie Fitzpatrick and Joann Murphy for their invaluable input in reading portions of the manuscript. I also want to thank, for their advice in regard to various parts of this book, Elizabeth Austin, Jane Lamson, and my sisters Mary Hurtig and Ellen Schrecker. Especially I want to thank my listeners — my wife, Mary Alice, and my friend Hugh Conlon, whose continuing willingness to hear fresh parts of this book was so essential to me during its production.

I am also in debt as always to my agent, Joseph Spieler, and my editor at Farrar, Straus and Giroux, Elisabeth Kallick Dyssegaard, whose support and confidence in what I do has always been greatly appreciated. Last I want to thank Wendy Friedman and Christine Scibelli, who put in many, many hours in the typing and retyping of my manuscript.

Contents

Contents

Contents

Contents

Contents

"Why did you have to get a divorce? And when can I get a hamster?"

Introduction

I have worked as a clinical psychologist for twenty-five years, mainly seeing children and teenagers. Reflecting the population at large, about half the kids that I have seen have been part of a divorce. What I have observed about kids and divorce is that their parents' divorce does become a huge part of their lives, but that their lives also do go on. Some not so well, but some quite well. It is what happens next, following the divorce, that, more than anything, ends up being the most important in the ultimate happiness of any given child.

A basic assumption of this book is that children are not necessarily—by the fact of divorce—doomed to a second-class childhood. They are not destined to grow up with a basic emotional lack. There is no question that many children, because of their parents' divorce, were damaged and were damaged in a way that never did completely come right. But nothing is written in stone. This book assumes that despite divorce there is much that remains within a parent's power that can yet determine whether their children and they with their children can have a nice life.

This book is a guide for parents who are going or have been through a divorce; it assumes that one natural parent no longer lives in the home, usually because of divorce. It is a guide to help those parents as best as possible try to make for their kids a childhood that can be as good as it can be. It is about—given divorce —what parents can do for their kids to create childhoods that can still nurture and produce healthy, happy children.

A major theme of this book is that if you want to help your kids to have as nice as possible lives, children of divorce that they are, you have one major role above all else: *During the time you are with them* you want to give them the love, caring, protection, being there for them no matter what, that are the essentials—and always will be—of what parents can do to produce healthy, happy kids.

This book is about the realities of divorce that can get in the way of a parent's being able to accomplish this relatively straightforward but not necessarily easy job. It is about how to help steer children through the pain and the complex of feelings that so often come with divorce, feelings that, if not resolved, can go forward in children's lives as a continuing cloud.

What do you say to kids when the divorce happens?

How can you help them deal with their first painful feelings of shock, confusion, sadness, betrayal, blame—all of which are inevitable?

How do you deal with the other parent, about whom both you and your kids still have very strong feelings?

How do you deal with your children when, as sometimes happens, that other parent gradually fades out of their lives?

How do you deal with the other parent who may be in their lives all too much?

How do you protect the kids from being caught in the middle of your disputes with the other parent?

How can you save them from being caught in that terrible snare of conflicting loyalties between two parents, both of whom they want and need to love, and by whom they want to be loved?

What do you do about all the new people who often come into your and your kids' lives after the divorce?

In what follows I will try to provide answers to these questions —and many more. Hopefully, starting with the most important factor of all—your love for and commitment to your children— this book will help make the rest of the time for you and your kids—despite divorce—a happy one.

1

Breaking the News

THEIR FIRST REACTION

I used to live with my family in a house that traveled through the air. And I never was afraid, because my house was big and strong. But today I heard a big crack and suddenly the house broke in two. Looking down over the edge, there was just empty space and I was very scared.

Children's first reaction to the news of their parents' divorce will most often be simple and straightforward.

What's going to happen? Am I going to be okay? I'm scared. I don't want them to get a divorce. I hate this. Maybe if I close my eyes this will all turn out to be a dream and go away.

The bottom has dropped out of their world. What they have always known and what they have always taken for granted—the basic structure of their lives—what they have always felt would magically make everything okay and protect them from all the terrors of the world—suddenly, all this is no more.

WHO SHOULD TELL THEM

When experiencing a major shock like this, children want to be with the person who makes them feel the safest. If one parent clearly has been in the main parenting role, that parent should break the news. Otherwise, which parent tells them might matter to the parents, but it means nothing to the children. The news itself is so huge that it bowls over everything else, including the messenger. Therefore, however you and your soon to be ex-spouse tell your kids, whatever you are both most comfortable with is fine.

WHEN TO TELL THEM

Several "whens" need to be considered in breaking the news. The first is that you should tell your children about the pending separation or divorce only after that particular decision is final. From your children's perspective, either you are splitting up or you are not. If you're unsure, do not "prepare them" for the possibility.

"Your father and I are thinking about getting a divorce."

Your advance warning only increases their worrying with no real benefit. It becomes a form of torture.

"Have you decided yet? Is it going to happen? When? Please don't. No. Please don't."

Well, yes, actually it is going to happen. Only I'm not telling you yet. Instead I'm drawing it out to make it easier for you.

No, thank you.

The second "when" is the actual time that you select to tell them. The news will be a big shock. They will need time to let it

When to Tell Them: Timing Is Important

sink in. Although there never is a good time, you need at least to make sure that the moment you select is one when you will be together for a while, preferably on a nonschool day. When they are suddenly feeling very unsafe and very alone, they will need you to be there for them, so they can feel as safe *as possible* and not *so* alone. When you or they are about to go off somewhere—to school, to work, to soccer practice—is not a good time to break the news. Just before bedtime is another bad choice. They probably wouldn't get to sleep for a long time after that bedtime story.

"Why did you have to get a divorce?"

What to Tell Them

"Your father and I have decided to get a divorce."

Use the word "divorce" if you have decided that you are getting a divorce. It's the word that the world uses, and you don't want to avoid it. If your children are very young and may not understand what divorce means, use the word, but also explain it.

"Which means that your father and I won't be married anymore. We won't be living in the same house anymore."

If you have decided to separate, but don't yet know about divorce, tell them that.

"Your father and I have decided that he is going to move out of the house for a while—he will be staying with Grandpa and Gramma."

"Why? Why's Daddy going?"

"We've decided that for now it's better this way."

"Are you going to get divorced?"

"We don't know. But for now Dad will be staying with Grandpa and Gramma."

Speculation about what may happen down the road can only pull children into additional worrying. Stick with what you do know and admit to that which you don't.

"Are you getting a divorce? You have to tell me. I have to know."

"For now, we just don't know."

After you've broken the initial news, tell your children what is going to happen to them. Keep whatever you say short and to the point. They are totally overwhelmed by the news they've just heard, so don't provide more details than they can handle. The basics are more than enough.

"You and Tricia will still live here with me. Your dad is moving out. He's going to live with Uncle Phil for a while. You will still get to spend time with him. We're not exactly sure yet how that will work out, but whatever happens, you will always have a home and you will always get to see both of us."

Telling Them Why

I don't care why they're getting a divorce. I hate all of this. This is a nightmare. I just want it to go away. I don't want them to get a divorce. I want it to go back to like it was before. I want to hide under a blanket and maybe when I come out they'll tell me it was all just a joke.

Initially, the news of the split-up floods out everything else. Children aren't interested in the reasons. Parents are mainly the ones who care about "why."

The kids need to know it wasn't my fault. I don't want them to blame me. I don't want them to be mad at me when it wasn't my choice at all. I wasn't the one who started having the affair and then decided to end the marriage. It's not fair to have them be mad at me for something that wasn't my fault at all. They need to know that.

No, they don't, not when they're first getting the news. They just want it all to go away. They may ask "Why?" but this "Why?" is not actually looking for reasons for the divorce.

"Why? Why are you getting a divorce? I don't want you to get a divorce. Why do you have to?"

This "Why?" really means "Why is this happening to me? I don't want it to happen. Tell me it's not going to happen." This "Why?" is asking if there is some way the situation can be undone. It is a plea for something that will instantly make the news of the divorce somehow more understandable and manageable. But at this moment nothing can—except time.

Unfortunately, at this time, explanations don't really help.

"I know this is hard for you to understand, but sometimes adults who were once in love find they don't love each other anymore. You know how your dad and I fought and argued a lot. Well, we just didn't love each other anymore. All the good feelings we had for each other were gone. We both felt that it would be best if we got a divorce."

Actually, this speech is not a bad one; at least it doesn't blame anybody. The problem is that when children first hear the news of the divorce, they simply aren't interested. However, if you feel you need to provide a reason, make it simple and not too informative, even if the actual reasons are complex or one-sided—as they often are.

"Your father and I were not getting along, so we have decided it would be best to get a divorce."

This tells them very little, but at this point that's all they need to know about the reasons. If you provide a simple statement, also make clear that there is nothing that they can do to change the situation. For example, note the "we have decided." It's very important to present a united stand. Mentioning that only one parent wants the divorce while the other doesn't opens up a huge can of worms. Since your kids don't want the divorce, they will latch on to this division immediately and see great hope in trying to convince the initiator of the action to change his or her mind.

"Please, Mommy, please. Give Daddy another chance. Daddy says he and you can work things out. You'll see. You have to give him at least one more chance—for us."

Don't give them this opportunity. They need to know the bottom line: it's happening and nothing is going to change this fact.

Anthony E. Wolf

After You Tell Them

"No, please, I don't want you to get a divorce. No, please. No."

They sob. Or perhaps they just sit there and say nothing. Whatever their reaction, once you tell them, be there. Be there to answer questions—if they have them. Be there to comfort them. Just be there. At this point, simply being with them is more important than anything else.

You may have some answers for their questions. You might want to offer some words of reassurance:

"You'll see. It won't be so bad. You'll get to see both of us. Lots of kids' parents get divorced. You know Jamie and Trish. Their parents are divorced and they're doing fine."

Such reassurances are nice if you want to give them, but in reality they're not going to make your kids feel much better. They're not ready to look on the bright side of anything yet. They're in shock. What they need most is your presence. And time.

For those children who react with stunned silence, you don't want to try too hard to draw out their feelings.

"You're not saying anything, William. You can tell me. How do you feel about it?"

How does he feel about it? He's very upset. That's how he feels about it. He probably doesn't feel like talking about it because he would burst into tears, which he apparently doesn't want to do, and his parents must respect this. Parents should let their kids react however they want and need to react.

What Else to Tell Them

As the news starts to sink in, even the quietest children probably will have questions. But they still can't take in a lot of information

"Why did you have to get a divorce?"

at one time, so your answers should always be short, honest, and as specific as possible.

"How much will I get to see Daddy?"
"We're not sure. But for now, we think it will be a couple of times a week."

"Will me and Tricia still live together?"
"I think so. For now you definitely will."

"Mommy, are you sad about the divorce?"
"Yes, the divorce makes me sad."

If you really don't know the answer to a question, it's always best to say that. Don't try to come up with an answer that in the end might be inaccurate.

"How much will I get to see Daddy?"
"I don't know. You will get to see him. But how much right now I don't know."
"But will it be enough?"
"I hope so."
"It will be a lot. Won't it?"
"I don't know."

Don't make promises that might not be kept. "I don't know" is almost always the right answer if you truly don't know. Kids may not like it, but answers for the sake of answers or just to put an end to the conversation always end up backfiring anyway.

"But you said . . ."

Well, actually I did. But I didn't mean it. I only said that so you would quit asking me.

2

Children's Reactions

THE FIRST WEEKS AND MONTHS

During the first weeks and months following the announcement, changes due to the impending divorce start to take effect. One or the other parent may leave, new daily routines may replace old ones, a parent may have to change work hours. And some previous unknowns and "I don't knows" may clarify themselves.

"You're going to stay weekends with your dad at Uncle Adam's house. Your dad will also come and take you out for dinner each Wednesday night."

However, some issues may remain unclear:

"I don't know. We might have to move. For now I just don't know. But if we have to move, it won't be anytime soon."

As children begin living with the huge new fact of life—"My parents are getting a divorce"—they also come to understand that life goes on, which is good to know. And they are able to *see*, as no words can tell them, what this does and does not mean in their day-to-day life.

"Dad never gets to put me to bed anymore."

"Mom worries about money a lot, which she didn't used to."

"We have to go over to a sitter's on Tuesdays and Thursdays because Mom had to switch her hours at work."

Some of the changes may not be so bad, but some will not be for the better. Yet as time passes, kids begin to notice one very reassuring fact: They are still here. They haven't fallen through a big hole in the world. They haven't died. Though their world was turned upside down and their lives are different now, nothing truly terrible has happened to them, and their initial terror begins to recede.

I don't like any of this. I don't like any of the changes. But Mommy's still Mommy, and Daddy's still Daddy, and Kyle's still a big jerk. And I'm still me.

TELLING THEIR FRIENDS

I don't know. I suppose I could tell Ricky and Glenn that my parents are getting divorced. But their parents aren't divorced. I don't know. I don't know what they'll say.
Do you think they would tease me? I think maybe I won't say anything.

Worrying about their friends' reactions is almost always a bigger problem than the actual reactions themselves. Kids used to get teased sometimes about having divorced parents, but divorce is so common today that the shame of being the child of divorce is not what it once was. But kids still worry about it anyway because they hate anything that makes them stand out from their peers. They fear that their friends will look at them differently in some manner because of the divorce. They worry that their parents' divorce will be like a big "D" stamped on their foreheads for all to see.

If your kids are worried about telling their friends, *encourage* them to do so.

"You'll see that once they know, you'll be happier. You don't want to carry it around like a secret. And once they know, you'll see how it's not a big deal."

If they need help with exactly what to say, tell them to say simply, "My parents are getting a divorce."

They'll see for themselves that once the news is out in the open, their worry will fade away.

"Sharon, I've got to tell you something."
"What?"
"My parents are getting a divorce."
"Oh, that's terrible, Deena. I feel so sorry for you. I sure hope mine don't. Did your parents argue a lot?"
"I don't know. I suppose. But I was real upset when they told me."
"Did you cry? I would've. Do you remember the time Christy Waterman started crying right in the middle of gym class? I'm sure glad we don't have Ms. Dishman for gym this year. She's too mean, don't you think?"

BLAME

With the hard fact that the divorce is for real comes the question of who is to blame, whose fault it is. Blame is the outward emotional response to the many bad feelings, mostly the sadness and anger, that surround a divorce. Some kids blame themselves, while

Telling Their Friends–Not Quite What They Fear

others blame one or both parents. Inevitably, *someone* will be blamed.

When They Blame Themselves

In regard to blame and your children, your first worry should always be: Do they blame themselves? Not all children blame themselves, but many do—and sometimes for reasons you would never dream of. Blame that would make no sense to you, or you have no clue where it came from, can be floating around in their heads.

I know I was bad a lot. They would always argue about what they should do to me. They never agreed. I always ran to Mom because I knew she was less strict than Dad about punishment. And that always made him extra angry. Now they're getting a divorce and it's all because of me. It's all my fault.

Or for less logical reasons:

I was real mad at them and I wished they'd get a divorce and I'd go live on an island. Now they're divorced. Maybe it's my wish come true. I didn't really want it, but it's too late. It's my fault.

Or simply:

I was bad a lot and this is God punishing me. It's all my fault.

Children can never handle either blame of this magnitude or the accompanying guilt of being the cause of their parents' divorce. If they carry this guilt with them over the years, they will have problems. So what do you do?

Let's say that the first scenario above was partially true. Prior to the divorce, a major problem had been a big rift between the mother and father over the handling of a particularly difficult child. Some kids will come right out and say it.

"It was because I was bad and you and Mom fought about it, wasn't it? It was my fault, wasn't it?"

Regardless of the reality, your answer has to be:

"No, it wasn't your fault. Yes, your mother and I disagreed. And yes, as you know, the fights were often about you. But we are not divorcing because of you or your behavior. We are getting divorced because your mother and I cannot live together."

"Because you fought so much about me being bad?"

"Yes, we fought about you. But the divorce is not about you. It's about your mother and me."

"And about me being bad."

They may keep trying to put it on their behavior, but you must always bring it back to you and your ex.

"No, it was not about you, it was about us."

As I said earlier, there are children who will suffer silently and who may think it was their fault but never say anything about it. How will you know if the silent ones blame themselves? Unless you ask, you won't. Therefore, because blaming themselves is such a common reaction and because it has the potential to do so much damage throughout the rest of their lives, you should ask your children if they blame themselves for the divorce.

"Do you sometimes worry that your dad and I are getting our divorce because of you? Do you sometimes worry that it was your fault?"

"No, I don't worry about that."

This is such an important issue, even if they say it's not an issue, even if it seems stupid to keep bringing it up, even if they appear totally disinterested (which maybe they really are), you must reinforce the fact that the divorce is not their fault. You never want them to live with the burden of that guilt.

"I just wanted you to know the divorce was not because of anything you did. What happened was between your mother and me."

"I know that. You've already told me that six times."

When They Blame You or Your Ex

Adults don't tolerate blame very well either. In fact, most people are wary about being blamed, even if it is about nothing at all.

"Were you the one who moved the sprinkler from the front lawn?"

"I don't know. Why?"

"Well, if you did, thanks. I was afraid someone might trip on it."

"Yeah, well, actually I did. I remember now."

Certainly, to be blamed for something as huge as a divorce, especially to be blamed by your kids whom you absolutely don't want to blame you seriously for anything, isn't something that any parent wants. But children will blame one or both of their parents, and, moreover, parents often get blamed when the divorce was neither their wish nor their initiative.

They blame me, but the whole thing was his fault. Why do I have to be the fall guy?

Even when a parent wanted and initiated the divorce, he or she often doesn't feel responsible for it.

I know I ended it. But I didn't do anything wrong in wanting the divorce. It was not my plan or my choice that the marriage went so badly. That's not what I wanted. I know I was far from perfect. But it was not my fault that in the end the only feelings left were bad ones.

Blaming one or both parents is one of the more loaded issues in a divorce.

"I hate you. The divorce is all your fault."

"Why did you have to get a divorce?"

Yet their blame is not quite what it seems. When kids place blame, they are not after some kind of deep condemnation of you, some historic acceptance of fault on your part, although this is how the accusation feels. Rather, kids are usually after something quite different and far more immediate. They just want to tell you how they feel.

"I'm mad at you. Don't you get it?"

Remember, assigning blame is really about hurt and anger. And, in fact, often they are blaming you not so much because they think it was your fault as because they feel bad and they have nobody else to blame.

I mean, I don't want to blame myself, because that makes me feel too awful. And I can't blame Dad, because he'd be too mad and maybe wouldn't ever see me again. So all that's left is Mom.

You make a mistake if you try to deflect the blame—or, for that matter, even to pick up on the blame issue at all. Any explanation only makes them feel that you are not hearing them. It's not useful to say things like:

"No, I know you feel it was my fault. But you'll understand when you get older. Marriage is very complicated . . ."

Recognizing and accepting their feelings is much more helpful.

"I know you feel bad about the divorce. I know you're mad at me."
"I do. The whole divorce is your fault and I'll never forgive you."

But they will. Right now, however, they want you to know how they feel. They want to tell you. They don't want you to do anything. They still love you. They just want you to know how they feel—sad and angry—and the easiest way to express this is through blame. They have to blame *someone*. It's a normal reaction. If you let them tell you how they feel, even though it's through blame, they'll feel better and their angry feelings will recede.

Children will outwardly blame only a parent whose love they're sure of. If they say they blame you, it is absolutely because they feel safe in doing so.

I can say anything to Mommy because I know she will always love me—no matter what I say.

Eventually, their deep love for you will lead them through this conflict between blame and love.

Inside the child, this is the conflict:

I love Mom, but I hate the divorce and it's her fault.

If we let them work through the blame question on their own without getting into it with them, without trying to defend ourselves, without doing anything, their love will, with time, win out over the blame.

Maybe the divorce was her fault, I don't know, but I can't seem to get mad about that anymore. I love her and I wish things were different, but they're not.

Blame can as easily fall on your ex as on you.

"I hate Daddy. He wrecked our family."

It can be so tempting to agree:

Nightmare #3

Well, she's right. That bastard did wreck our family. He wrecked her childhood and he wrecked my life. I don't see why I shouldn't let her know how it was.

"Honeybiscuits, I don't want to say anything against your father, but he is the most dishonest, self-centered, coldhearted man that ever lived. Now, I don't want you to think badly of him or blame him for the divorce, but the divorce was totally because of him and his slimy, heartless ways."

But it is never good, no matter how tempting. Much better is simply not to touch the blame issue at all.

"I know you feel bad about the divorce."
"I do. Dad's a jerk. And I'm always going to hate him for the rest of my life for what he did to us."

Maybe she will, but probably she won't. It's best to stay out of it. There's not even any need to defend her father.

"No, the divorce is not your father's fault. We simply could not work things out between us."
"No, it was him. He's a jerk."

Again, the same rules apply as with blaming you. If you don't get into it with her, she can work through her feelings for her father on her own. Their relationship will then play itself out based on what goes on only between them, which is the way it should be.

Blame and Betrayal

With the question of blame, you don't want to forget one fact. Deep inside all kids whose parents get divorced lies a very genuine anger at, and sense of betrayal by, *both* parents, regardless of whom they claim to blame. Their parents have broken a birthright contract that says they will always stay together for their children.

They're not allowed to get a divorce. If they had me, they have to stay together. That's part of the deal. If you have kids, you have to stay married. It's not fair to the kids to get a divorce.

All children of divorce feel this at some level and, as with the other types of blame we've discussed, trying to defend yourself or your ex will only make things worse.

Some Things Are Hard to Resist

"Well, you know the world isn't always perfect. Things don't always work out as you want them to."

"They did until you got a divorce."

They have a right to their feelings, so let them be angry.

Blame That Doesn't Fade

Some blame doesn't go away, even with the passage of time. It's usually blame that's specifically attached to the perceived reason for the divorce. Where one parent clearly caused the divorce, or where one parent wanted the divorce and the other didn't, a child's blame can hang on for quite a while, especially if the parent who was left behind or who didn't want the divorce falls apart.

"Dad divorced Mom to be with Louise and he's been happy. But it ruined Mom's life. She's never been the same since Dad left."

What should a parent do if the ex-spouse has an overly difficult time in the aftermath and becomes a continuing worry and source of sadness for the kids? Again, explanations and self-serving defenses are mistakes. They only make matters worse. The best course is to accept the fact that the decision did create a real problem for your kids. And that your decision was made with eyes wide open.

"I know my leaving your mother made it hard for you. I know that you worry about her."

You're not exactly offering an apology, but you acknowledge that your actions created a problem for your children—an honest statement of a fact of life. They may never completely forgive you—

Mom's not a happy person. I don't know if she's ever going to be. And I think that wouldn't have happened if Dad hadn't left her.

—but they'll find a way to keep this fact from standing in the way of a good relationship with you.

I'll never totally forgive Dad for what he did to Mom because I'll always feel bad for Mom. But I love Dad anyway. I'm not mad at him. But so long as Mom is unhappy, I can't forget why.

Grieving over the Divorce

As time passes and they realize that the divorce really is forever, all children will grieve. Some will do it outwardly, fussing and crying—

"I hate the divorce. I miss Daddy. Why can't you get back together? Why?"

—and for them, as always, the best course is not to try to provide soothing answers. You can't. Just listen and be there for them.

"I know you feel bad about the divorce."
"I do. I hate it. I hate it."

Others will suffer silently but their grief is just as real and heartfelt as that of those who react openly. It can be easy to ignore them, but parents must be careful to be there for silent sufferers as well. Occasionally, in a quiet moment, go to them and ask:

"How do you feel about the divorce?"

Or:

"You feel bad about the divorce, don't you?"

In response, they may or may not open up to you:

"It's okay. I'm getting used to it."

But don't be fooled. It's always good to sometimes state what you know has to be in their hearts, even if they don't want to talk about it.

"Kevin, I know you don't say anything. But I know that you feel bad about the divorce, and I want you to know that I'm sorry that it had to happen."

Saying it for them does help. They know that you understand, and that they are not so alone with their sadness.

Divorce at Different Ages

"Harold and I hate each other. But we have decided that we'll stay together for the next three years until Rochelle is twelve and Darren is ten. We both feel that by then they will be a little older and the divorce will have a less deleterious effect on the two of them."

In general, at what age will a separation and divorce have the least damaging effect? The answer, of course, is that there is no best age. However, the effects of divorce on children do vary with their age, and parents need to understand those different effects and the differing needs of their children. Here are the more basic differences according to age.

0 to 2 Years Old

"Rafael, I have something important to tell you. Your mother and I are getting a divorce."

One-month-old Rafael continues to look at his father as he always does. That is, he continues to *sort of* look at his father because he's too young to focus well on things or people.

In the earliest stages of life, a child's perception of a divorce is obviously limited. Certainly infants have no real awareness of a divorce. The effects of a divorce on their lives—mainly, not growing up living in the same home with both their biological parents—will be in the future.

The number one psychological issue of child development is the formation of a strong special attachment to a main nurturing person or persons in a child's life. Children need regular ongoing contact with at least one continuing caregiver in order to make the initial, basic love attachment. This attachment becomes the foundation both of their sense of well-being—I am loved and special—and of their capacity for love in the future. Fortunately, in most divorces where very young children are involved, the presence of at least one loving parent—that most important of all requirements—does not get significantly disrupted.

However, the prospect of having two involved parents for children of this age becomes less likely. Obviously, following most separations one of the parents is no longer in the home on a regular basis and no longer has daily contact with the child. The result is that one parent, who, had the marriage continued, would have had more of an ongoing bond in both directions—child to parent and parent to child—does not have such a bond.

The risk that comes with this loss of daily contact with the second parent at such an early age is that this parent can swiftly and perhaps permanently fade out as a major factor in a child's life.

"I would have been happy to have him more involved with Michael and would have loved some babysitting from him. But it didn't happen."

If the ex does stay involved with the very young child, sometimes the main parent may worry about the care provided.

He doesn't have the daily experience with Lucinda. He doesn't know her needs. She's so little and so vulnerable.

He will learn. The same concerns come up when parents—divorced or not—entrust their child's care to anyone not a member of the immediate family. But this is a member of the immediate family—a full parent—and whether your ex is a skilled burper or diaper changer is not really the issue for your child. A loving parent is the issue. Keeping the contact going with your ex, encouraging it, and helping to make it easier is in your child's best interest and can be a major lifetime gain.

2 to 5 Years Old

"Yesterday we were at the pool and Anthony [three years old], who always loves to play with the other children in the kiddy pool, spent the whole time never more than two inches away from me. I don't understand. He's always been so independent. But lately, since his mother and I separated, he won't leave my side."

With a divorce or separation, toddlers and preschoolers are very aware that a major change has taken place. One or the other parent no longer lives at home—is no longer present in the expected places or at the expected time. Toddlers notice the loss.

"Why doesn't Mommy live here anymore? I miss Mommy. I want Mommy back."

When one parent leaves, another, greater terror lurks in the back of their mind:

If Mommy left, maybe Daddy will leave too.

With toddlers and preschoolers, the major divorce issues are change and loss. They don't like either because both are scary. Their confidence, their sense of trust that what they have will always be there, has taken a blow. A crack has opened in the foundation of their security. Their main response to this loss of confidence is to pull back within themselves and, as a result, the more outgoing features of their personality can suffer. They are more reluctant to take chances. They cling to whatever security they still have, trying to make sure that nothing further happens to what remains. They don't leave your side to play in the kiddy pool.

For their confidence to reestablish itself, they will need time. Meanwhile, they'll need the reassurance that you are still there and not going to leave them.

"I know your Mommy doesn't live with us anymore. But I will always be here."

Your children might seem too young to understand all the changes that are happening, but you should still give them the same kind of simple explanations you would give kids of any age. It will make the changes in their lives a little easier on them if you tell them exactly what is going to happen.

"You and Tiffany are going to stay here with me. Mom is going to live at Grandma Becky's house. You'll get to see her a lot."

But at this age, even after reassurances and explanations, they can still be perplexed.

"But why? Why doesn't Mommy live here anymore? I want her back."

Again, they're not really asking for explanations, which you can give:

"Me and Daddy weren't happy living together. You remember how we yelled at each other a lot."

What they really want is for everything to go back to the way it was. Which is not going to happen. So if they become—for a while—fearful and clingy, let them.

6 to 12 Years Old

Once kids reach school age, the biggest issues that separation and divorce pose for kids of any age—the shock, the loss, and the uncertainty—are far from being the only issues. By the age of six, because of their increased awareness, new issues enter the picture. Issues such as guilt, blame, worrying about the welfare of a parent, worrying about money, being caught in the middle between two still-feuding parents—all these may become a part of everyday life. They find themselves right in the middle of their own soap opera and are very aware of all that has happened and will go on happening, and they have lots of thoughts about these events as well.

The prominent issue for younger school-age kids is that they are vulnerable to problems arising from conflicting loyalties to their divorced parents.

The score in the soccer game was tied 1–1. Nine-year-old Tiffany, a fullback, had been playing well. But with four minutes left, she slipped, allowing an opposing player to get past her and score. Her team lost 2–1. At the game's end, as soon as the coach dismissed the players, Tiffany, who always put considerable pressure on herself, burst into tears and ran across the field to where her mother and younger brother had been watching from the sidelines. As Tiffany sobbed, "I blew it. I blew it," her mother gave her a big hug.

Tiffany's father, standing on the sideline on the other side of the field near Tiffany's team bench, watched silently.

The next evening when Tiffany and her brother went to their father's for supper and to spend the night, her father commented on the previous afternoon.

"I'm sorry you were so upset. I thought you had played a good game. It wasn't your fault that you slipped. That could happen to anybody. You're a good player, Tiffany, and I'm proud of you. I did feel a little stupid, though, when you ran across the field to your mom, since I was standing there right next to you and your team."

Three weeks later Tiffany's team, which had won the rest of their regular-season games, was in the playoffs. With Tiffany playing brilliantly, her team won 1–0 on a late goal. At the end of the game, everyone on the team, including Tiffany, was jumping and hugging and yelling. However, when the players broke to go over to their families, Tiffany hung around the bench until her parents came over to her. She was not about to offend anybody by rashly letting her enthusiasm inadvertently show favoritism to either of her parents.

Because school-age kids have the double vulnerability of caring about loving and being loved by both parents, because they have a new cognizance of all that goes on around them, parents have to be sensitive to all the issues and conflicts that might affect them. Once children reach this age, parents can no longer safely assume:

"Oh, they're still too young to understand or worry about that."

Now, parents had better assume they will understand, because their children, like Tiffany, can and will be pulled into and suffer from these conflicts.

Teenagers

To most teenagers, the divorce of their parents is both a shock and an intrusion. Their own lives revolve around the very real and tough issues of adolescence—how do I fit in? what do I do about sex, drugs, and drinking?—as well as those smaller but very important issues of acne, what to wear to school, and teachers they don't like. They find it hard enough holding their own lives together. They definitely don't want to be bothered with the lives of their parents, which are now unraveling with the divorce. They have neither the room nor the time for the kind of disruption that divorce brings into their lives.

Besides, teenagers are a breed apart. They're not simply a few years older than their earlier selves. They're psychologically different. Though still dependent on their parents, they now have a strong inner voice telling them to become independent and begin to make a life of their own. It's no longer acceptable for them to depend on their parents for their sense of security and well-being.

"Screw you, I don't need either of you. I would do just fine living in an apartment on my own."

But that is the paradox of adolescence. Teenagers aren't independent; they only feel that they must be. And therein lies the main problem of divorce for teenagers. Though they're moving away from their parents, seeking more independence, they want and need to do this while still knowing that their parents are there if they need them.

"Actually, I don't mind living at the house, it's just that I don't like it when *they're* at home. I mean, I wouldn't want anything to happen to them. It's just that I would prefer if they didn't talk to me."

They want and need a home that they can count on despite the fact that at any given moment they may despise that home and the parent or parents in it, or even run away from it. A divorce undermines all of that, disrupting the base of security they need in order to face all the issues of adolescence. It produces a *forced* independence and a *real* growing up that no teenager ever truly wants.

What they want is separation and independence from their parents, but on their own terms:

"I'm going out. I'm not telling you where and I'll be back when I feel like it. But please make sure my two sweaters get to the cleaners."

The whole divorce issue may be much more volatile with teenagers because adolescence is also a time when they may be engaged in serious battles with one or both parents. Some of these can be loud and nasty. Divorce can both add to and complicate them.

"I don't care if they get a divorce. I hate them both. All they've been doing lately is trying to make my life miserable. They won't let me do anything I want. They keep badgering me about stuff that is totally stupid. I really don't care what they do."

But they do care and consequently their feelings can get very complicated.

If I hate them so much, how come I'm so upset about the divorce? How come I'm worried about them when I don't even like thinking about them?

Like younger kids, adolescents can and will get caught up in all of the more complex issues of divorce, and they are influenced by what one or the other parent might say.

"Carlton, you can't imagine how much your father has hurt me going off with that slut Lisa."

However, they are also more independent thinkers and often form their own opinions about what has gone on. These opinions can be incredibly intense, perhaps shortsighted, as well as very moral and condemnatory—especially when it comes to a parent whom they feel has been wronged and whom they feel is especially hurting and vulnerable.

"Hi, Kevin. Is it okay if I come over Wednesday night and pick
you up and you and I can go out for supper?"

"No."

"What do you mean 'no'?"

"No. I don't know what you're thinking, Dad. But if you think
you can just go off with Lisa and do what you've done to Mom,
and I'm supposed to pretend that nothing has happened, you're
wrong."

Divorced parents of teenagers need to keep clearly in mind that
whatever is going on between them and their teenage child, or
between their ex and their teenager, will often fade away by the
end of adolescence. Adolescence is a stage: it comes and it goes.
Many of its passions are transitory. Teenagers can hate and then
no longer hate at all. Their feelings about issues that seemed so
black and white, so absolute, somehow change.

"I mean, Dad was a total jerk and an asshole. He really was. I
mean, he still is. But he is my father. I mean, I don't want to go
around hating my father my whole life. I know he loves me. He's
just an asshole, that's all. But I love him."

Reunited Parents: The Eternal Dream

Seven-year-old Robert to his father:

"Dad, Mom said that if you want to come straight from work to
pick us up Friday night, it's okay with her. Even though you'll be
getting there a little before Jamie gets dropped off after her soccer
game. But Mom said that you can wait around at the house with
me and her and that that's okay with her until Jamie is home and
then you can take us."

*I mean, you never know. If Mom and Dad are there together,
they'll probably talk, and you never know. Maybe if they talk and*

Kids Never Give Up

it's nice they can start to like each other again. And you never know, maybe they'd end up spending more time together. And you never know. It could happen, maybe they'd get back together again. It could happen.

This hope, that the separation is temporary and the divorce itself may still not happen, that one's parents will get back together, is always alive. Not only does the hope stay alive, but there often can be a continuing fantasy of how wonderful it had been and could be again, even though maybe it never really was.

Two Christmas Memories

"You want your parents to get back together?"

"Oh yeah, I do."

"But I thought they fought violently all the time and the police constantly came to the house and you were always hiding in the closet."

"Yeah, well, the closet wasn't so bad. It was a nice closet. I liked it in the closet. Besides they loved each other."

"They did?"

"Yeah, Dad once brought Mom a souvenir glass from the bar he always went to after they fought."

"Why did you have to get a divorce?"

"But you told me she threw it at his head."
"Yeah, but it missed."

All children wonder about a reconciliation. Some will even ask you directly. But if they don't ask and you're certain the separation is permanent, you need to state the facts every once in a while. A reality check helps keep this futile dream in perspective.

"I know you don't ask, but the divorce is going to happen. Your father and I are not going to get back together. This is the way it's going to be."

Even years after the divorce, this hope can still live in some secret place:

Well, I know all they did was fight and they still hate each other, and it probably is better this way. But maybe, I mean maybe they could get to like each other. And we could be a family again—even though actually we never were much of a family. Maybe someday we could be. It would be so nice. It would be perfect.

3

Reacting to Their Reactions

HOW TO TALK AND LISTEN

Perhaps the hardest part is knowing what to say to them. Not just in presenting the separation or divorce, but in responding to all they may say and do. One of the keys is knowing how to listen and talk. It turns out that the solution to many seemingly complex and difficult issues can be found in the simpler here and now of the ways in which parents talk and listen to their kids in general. Your success in helping your children work through the many and various hurts, losses, sadnesses, changes, disruptions, and inconveniences caused by the divorce is *not* contingent upon knowing the answers for everything.

"But I don't want to move. Tell me we won't have to move. I don't want to go to a new school. I don't want to have to make new friends. I like my old friends. Tell me we won't have to move. Tell me."

"What are you talking about, Richard? I haven't said anything about moving."

"But Jimmy Oberman's parents got divorced and he had to

move. Tell me we won't have to move. Promise me, Mommy. Promise me we won't have to move."

What do I say to him? I don't want to lie to him. I don't plan to move, but who knows what's going to happen. I could meet some-body. Money could become a problem. I could have to change jobs. What do I say?

Or Sarah to her mother:

"But why did you and Dad have to get a divorce? Why? I hate it. I hate the divorce. Why won't you and Daddy get back to-gether?"

"Your father and I weren't happy together. It just didn't work out."

"But what about me? I'm not happy. Don't I count?"

"We thought it would be best for everybody, including you. Your dad and I did not get along. That's not good for us and that's not good for you."

"Yes, it is. I don't care if you fought. I liked it better before. I want you back together."

How do I get out of this? I can't seem to come up with the right answer. Everything I say to her only seems to make it worse. She just throws it back at me. I can't seem to come up with an answer that satisfies her, that makes things any better.

What do you say to them? How do you answer seemingly un-answerable questions? Fortunately, there are some rules for talking and listening that can and do help.

Keep It Short and Simple

When talking to your kids, long complicated answers and reassur-ances simply do not work. Your good intentions to close off all possibilities of concern and worry will more often leave your kids neither satisfied nor reassured. They'll just pick up on something you say and use it as another point to take off from.

"You really don't need to worry about whether we move. As far as I know, we're not going to move. But if we do, I would make sure that it was a place that we were all happy with."

"But would it be as nice as this? Would it be farther away from Dad? What about all my friends?"

If you try to answer all of these worries, you're stuck with having to get into further hypothetical detail.

"Well, if we didn't move too far, I'd make sure that you still get to see all your friends. Maybe not as much as before, but you'd still see them. And you'll see, wherever we move you'll be able to make new friends."

"How do you know I'll be able to make new friends? How do you know that?"

No sooner have you plugged one worry hole with a reassurance than a new one springs up. Rather than seal off children's fears and worries, complex reassurances tend to continue and expand them. So it's better to give clear, short, simple answers focused on the present.

"I don't know if we'll ever move. But for now, I know that we're not moving."

"But if we did move, what would happen?"

"I don't know. But I do know that for now, we're not moving."

"But you have to tell me that we'll never move. You have to. I won't sleep."

If you stay firm, focused on the here and now, you help them stay in the present and limit their own fears and worries about what may or may not happen.

"Why did you have to get a divorce?"

"I don't know about 'never,' but for now we're not moving."

By closing the issue, you allow them to move on.

I don't know what's going to happen if we move. But maybe I'll worry about that tomorrow. "Mom, what's for lunch?"

Or this scenario:

"Promise me you won't get married again."
"No, I can't promise. But I'm not planning on getting married anytime soon."
"But *promise* me. You have to promise me. I don't want you to get married again to anybody but Daddy."
"I know you feel bad about the divorce. But it's possible, not now, but maybe someday, that your father or I could get married again. After all, some parents remarry. But that's not going to happen anytime soon, and if it ever did, you would still always have me."

That's not a bad statement, in theory, but in practice it doesn't work very well. The response you would hope to get from your child might be something like

"Well, it would make me sad, but so long as I always have you, I guess it's okay."

The response you would more likely get would be:

"Then you *are* going to get married again. But I don't want you to. Promise me. You have to promise me. Don't get married again."

It's better to stay with the short, simple, in-the-present answer.

"But promise me. You have to promise me. I don't want you to get married again to anybody but Daddy."

"No, I can't promise. But I'm not planning on it anytime soon."

"But you have to promise me. You have to."

"No, but I'm not getting remarried anytime soon."

Stay firm and their concerns will have a way of running out of steam.

Be Honest

If you don't know, say so. What you don't want to do is promise what might not be true. The truth is almost always best even if, at the time, it seems awkward and you're tempted to be evasive. Anything that is, or may be, untrue can and usually will come back to haunt you.

"You hate Daddy, don't you?" asks Carla, who has repeatedly witnessed that this is very clearly the case.

"No, I don't hate your father. It is just that the divorce has been difficult."

Better the truth:

"That's right, I don't like your father. I don't like him a lot."

But doesn't her mother's saying she doesn't like Carla's father make Carla feel that if she wants her mother to like her, she's supposed to dislike her father too? Not at all. Her mother's answer obligates Carla to nothing. She is still free to like her father—provided Carla's mother makes no demands on Carla to feel as she does. Being honest keeps communication between Carla and her mother at the most helpful level—away from half-truths and needless complexities. Each degree of not being honest is one degree further away from children's feeling that they can speak as they want and truly be heard.

What if they ask you a question that you really do not want to answer? You don't have to answer.

"Did you leave Daddy because you liked somebody else?"

Which you did, but you are no longer involved with that person and do not feel it is something you want your child to know about. You can always say,

"That's not something I will talk about."
"You did, didn't you?"

But hang in there. Make it clear that this is a subject you simply will not discuss.

"That's not something I will talk about."
"But why?"
"It's not something I will talk about."

If you're firm, they'll accept that some subjects are closed, and ultimately they'll back off.

Hearing What They Say

To go back to Sarah's discussion with her mother.

"But why did you and Dad have to get a divorce? Why? I hate it. I hate the divorce. Why won't you and Daddy get back together?"

Very often the best response to much of what kids say is to listen. Many questions and even what might seem like personal attacks are rather their way of telling you how they feel. Just that and no more. They want to feel heard and understood. Even though it may not seem that that's what they are after.

What parents invariably discover is that it is a mistake to try to soften or deflect the impact of what their kids say, to somehow try to make it all better. Hence, saying soothing things may seem like a good idea.

"I know you hate the divorce. But you'll see, things will get better. It won't be nearly as bad as you think."

But children experience such responses as your not hearing what they are saying. Sarah wants her mother to know—in no uncertain terms—that she hates the divorce.

"Didn't you hear me? I said I hate the divorce."

Except that they don't say it that way. They say,

"No, it won't be better. I know. You're wrong. It'll never get better. It's gonna ruin my life."

Often what they want from their parents is not answers because no answer their parents would give would be what they really want to hear. The only answer that would actually satisfy Sarah would be,

"Oh, okay. If you really feel so bad about the divorce, your father and I will call it off."
"You will?"

Just as, when they are mad about the divorce, they don't want to hear any defense you might try to counter their anger with. It is not useful to say things like

"Well, don't be mad at me about the divorce. It was not my choice. It was not something I wanted."

In response to your children's angry words, you probably will feel that you need to do something. But the only thing you need to do is listen. By simply listening, you show them that you understand, that you recognize and accept their feelings, and that you're not blown away by their angry words, even if that may hurt some. You hear them and you let them have their bad feelings. That's part of being a good parent. It helps them. It makes them feel better. And they do love and appreciate you for it.

It is an important point. Almost always the best responses are short, honest, and to the point and simply reflect that you understand how they feel.

"Why did you have to get a divorce? It's so stupid. It ruins everything. Why did you have to?"
"I know you feel bad about the divorce."
"I do. I hate it. I hate the divorce."

Sarah is relieved and thankful that her mother hears her.

Counseling Can Help—Parents and Kids

In any divorce situation, counseling can be useful. When problems or questions arise, when you simply do not know what to do, counselors, because they have experience, can help. They can offer not just support, but good concrete suggestions about how to handle tough situations in this new territory. My experience has been that kids, both teens and grade schoolers, like counseling. They can take advantage of a neutral situation to talk about their concerns and say things that they would hesitate to say to their parents.

"I don't like Dad's girlfriend, Elizabeth, and when I told Dad one time all he did was get mad at me, so I never said it again. If I talk about it to Mom, she gets mad at Dad. She actually called him one time to complain about Elizabeth and she and Dad had this screaming fight on the phone. It was a big mess, which wasn't what I wanted. I know Dad is going to keep seeing Elizabeth. It's just that I don't really like her and I can't say it to either Mom or Dad without some huge reaction."

Moreover, counseling *should* be sought for kids when they are clearly having a hard time with the divorce. If they seem continually upset and don't pull out of it, if school performance and school behavior fall off significantly and stay that way, if they seem noticeably less interested in friends and activities, or if they become much more argumentative and belligerent with you, with friends, or at school than they had been before the divorce, you should seek counseling for your kids.

In some circumstances, parents should seek counseling for themselves as well. If for whatever reason you are feeling overwhelmed, and that feeling doesn't go away, counseling can make a difference. Staying overwhelmed is no help to anybody—you or your kids.

Whom should you see? Psychologists, psychiatrists, social workers, and licensed counselors usually have experience in helping families with divorce. If you do not know of specific counselors or counseling centers (most towns have one of some kind reasonably nearby), ask. Your family doctor or pediatrician, guidance counselors at your children's school, or even an area hospital are good resources for referrals.

What You Can't Undo

Gwenette was eleven and her brother Randy was eight when their mother left, moving in with the man with whom she had been having an affair for the past two years. Unknown to the two children, their parents' marriage had been rocky for a number of years. Their parents had fought, but not excessively. However, the deeper problem, the lack of love and the growing bitterness in their relationship, wasn't seen by the kids. Both parents had done their best to make their home one in which their two children could grow and feel both happy and loved. They had succeeded.

Gwenette and Randy never dreamed that their parents would separate or thought that their childhoods would change so dramatically and forever. But the unthinkable had happened and their lives would never be the same. The night their mother moved out, their father explained what had happened. In the ensuing days Gwenette and Randy talked with their mother and more or less began to understand. They would stay at the house with their father and see their mother regularly. As time went on, Gwenette and Randy got used to the new day-to-day pattern of their lives, but at night they would sometimes cry quietly to themselves, each with a feeling that was strange and cold.

I want it to go back to the way it was before.

They remember how it was, and now inside them comes this new place of emptiness. This hole. Because the way it used to be isn't anymore.

If divorce and its consequences cause kids to suffer, how can parents help their children deal with that suffering? What can parents do so that the suffering doesn't turn into damage?

You cannot *undo* the true bad that comes into your children's lives. You cannot, with just the right words, with just the right acts of deep love and caring, make it all better. Bad feelings from bad things are real and cannot be washed away. But they can be shared, which in the end is the best way for you to help your children put their bad feelings to rest. In doing so, they do not feel so alone.

Be with them and let them know you care. And when it is just the two of you—alone—you might try to find the opportunity to say,

"I'm sorry. I know that the divorce made you unhappy and I'm sorry. I'm very sorry."

This "sorry" is not about fault or blame, but about their feelings. Left unsaid yet what they hear is:

"I'm sorry that what you wanted and what you had every right to expect—that you would be a kid in a family with both your mom and your dad—got wrecked. I'm sorry that things did not turn out how you wanted. I'm sorry that I failed to stop that from being taken away from you. I am truly sorry."

Your Most Important Role

Your influence on the ultimate welfare of your children is all about what happens when they are with you. If you are good and loving during that time, if you are someone whom they can consistently count on, then, divorced or not, you have done the single most important thing that any parent can do for his or her children. Your relationship with your child is what matters.

Focus on what goes on when you are with them. Make that time as good as it can be. But as anyone who has been there knows, somehow it is not at all as simple as it may sound.

4

The Long-Term Effects of Divorce

DOES DIVORCE RUIN A LIFE?

Years later, looking back as an adult:

I never really recovered from my parents' divorce. There I was going along, having a happy childhood, I mean except for normal stuff like my third-grade teacher, Mrs. Hildebrand, and Stevie Lesniak, who always made fun of my ears, and a certain problem about wet sheets at night that I would rather not discuss. And then in the middle of fifth grade my parents announce that they're getting a divorce and my dad moves out and that was it.

It really was a big shock. I knew they argued a lot. But so did most parents that I knew of. I just never dreamed that they would get a divorce.

I've always felt it was like somebody came in and picked up my life like it was a paper airplane, scrunched it all up, and then handed it back to me and said, "Okay, here's your life back, have fun." It just got wrecked.

Things just never were the same. Everything got worse. Instead of a nice life I started having a lousy life. I'm not sure what I was like before, but I certainly became a lousy kid. And I was so mad at my parents—which was hard because I still loved them and still needed them. But I was mad at them all the time.

I never got over it. I mean, I had some good times, but mainly I didn't. I didn't do as well in school as I should have. I haven't been able to find a job that really is any good. And I just don't seem to do very well in relationships. They start out okay, but then stuff goes wrong and I don't know what happens, but they never work out.

I wish somebody would give me my nice life back. But I guess that's not going to happen. I just feel it got taken away from me back in fifth grade.

Much has been written about the overall effect of divorce on kids. There is general agreement that in the long run divorce can definitely have a negative effect, and that it increases the chances that the rest of a child's life may not be as nice as it might have been. All divorced parents worry that their divorce will in some serious way not just hurt their kids in the time immediately following the divorce—which it will—but also cause permanent damage, possibly transforming a life that would have been okay into one that is not. Certainly, there are many men and women for whom their parents' divorce led to psychological scarring. But for any given child that damage is not certain. Moreover, not all agree that in the long run divorce is necessarily always bad for certain children. Many argue that the misery and tension between parents who chose to continue a failed marriage would have had at least as bad an effect on the kids as the divorce and its aftermath.

With any single life, it's hard to know which decision would have been better for all concerned. Without access to time machines and to parallel universes where comparisons could be made between the two stories—one where the parents stay together and one where they get a divorce—this is an argument that can never get totally resolved. For example:

"Why did you have to get a divorce?"

Clarence I from Parallel Universe I, whose parents stayed together, is now sixty years old and being interviewed.

"On a scale of one to one hundred, where one hundred is best, how, overall, would you rate your life?"

"A seventy-eight, definitely a seventy-eight. Basically a pretty good life, I'd say. Some downs, but what do you expect?"

Clarence II of Parallel Universe II, whose parents divorced when he was eight, interviewed at sixty:

"On a scale of one to a hundred how would you rate your life?"

"That's a hard one. But I guess I'd say it's been a twenty-eight. Not so good. A lot of heartache."

Finally, conclusive proof that divorce ruins a life. But, of course, we can't know ahead of time what will be a divorce's effect. However, two facts about divorce are hard to dispute. One, many adults are seriously scarred by their parents' divorce, end up having significantly worse lives, and turn out to be far less emotionally solid than they would be if there had been no divorce. Two, many adults who are the products of divorce are fine today. That is, divorce can cause long-term problems, but it doesn't have to.

Bad Effects You Can't Control

One frequent result of divorce is that the actual circumstances of your children's lives change for the worse. Commonly, money becomes a problem. The same amount now has to go further. Often where one parent is dependent on the other for financial assistance (child support), the money available to run the household is significantly less than it used to be.

"Why can't we ever go out to McDonald's anymore?"

"Why do I have to stop my dance lessons?"

For various reasons, a family may have to move. The move can mean that your kids have to go to a new school, thereby losing friends and having to make new friends all over again. Also the new home might not be as nice as where the family lived before.

"I don't like sharing my room with Charles—he's a slob. I don't like our new neighborhood either. It's not as nice as where we used to live."

The good news is that children are very adaptable and can handle a lot of change in their lives without suffering permanent damage. They often do better than their parents. They may even do well in seemingly adverse circumstances.

"I liked it better when we had more money, but I don't actually care a lot. I know Mom cares, and I feel bad when I can't get new sneakers all the time like some of my friends can. But I mean it's not like it ruins my life."

Still, some changes truly are bad. And some of these changes caused by the divorce—if you have to move and the kids lose long-time friends, or if they lose much or all of one parent's presence—will have a negative impact on the kids' lives, no way around it.

"Dad moved to Florida and I haven't seen him in a year and a half. And he only calls on Christmas and my birthday."

"Since Dad got married to Lorraine, we don't get to go over there much. He seems to care more about her kids and their baby Jeremy than about us."

What can you do about these bad consequences that are out of your control? You can't do anything. You and your kids are stuck with them. What should you do? Grieve for what's irredeemably bad and then go on and work on what you can change.

WHEN PARENTS FALL APART

"Mommy, can I get a Diamondbacks sweatshirt like Jimmy Millen? I don't think they cost a lot of money, Mommy."

"Yes, I guess so. I don't know. Maybe. You should ask your father the next time you're with him. I don't know, dear."

"Mommy, why are you crying?"

"I don't know, Henry. It's all so difficult since Daddy left."

"I'm sorry, Mommy. You're still sad about Daddy leaving, aren't you?"

I try to be cheerful. But I don't do a very good job. Since their father left I've just fallen apart. They see me crying. They know I'm upset. I'm not fun for them like I was before. I don't have the patience with them either, and I snap at them more. It has to hurt them. I feel real bad for them, but I don't know what to do about it.

Following a divorce, many parents become transformed from loving, confident mothers and fathers into emotional wrecks. Although they try to keep up a strong front, it is often very hard. And like the mother above, they worry that they are hurting their kids.

For children, it doesn't help when, on top of their own trauma from the divorce, one of their parents is noticeably weaker than before. Yet it often happens, and when it does, they react.

Sometimes kids can be very solicitous of emotionally upset parents.

"Don't worry about making supper, Mommy. I'll make it tonight."

"You can't. You don't know how to cook."

"I can make toast. We can have jelly toast for supper."

A nice gesture, but worrisome as well, because you don't want to cede your parenting role to your children.

When kids sense that one or both parents are not as strong as they used to be, they also will become anxious. They need their former strong parent, and their anxiousness causes them to try to get him or her back. So while they may be sweet and solicitous at times, at other times they will push. The easiest way for them to see their parents show some strength is to give them a hard time.

"But why? Why do I have to take a bath? I'm clean. I am. Why do I have to? Why? Why?"

"Justin, why can't you just take your bath? I don't understand why you're giving me such a hard time."

"I'm not giving you a hard time. I don't want to take a bath. I don't."

It would be nice if you could say, under these circumstances,

"The divorce has been very hard on all of us. And you know that it's been very hard on me. I'll get better, but right now I do get more easily upset than I used to. For now, I really need you to be more cooperative and not give me a such hard time."

And it would nice if they responded,

"Yes, Mommy. We know. We'll really try."

But unfortunately the response is more likely to be:

"I *am* being more cooperative. It's just that Trisha keeps bothering me and she never does any of her stuff."

Parents who find themselves emotionally weaker after a divorce don't need to worry if their kids see them upset, because their kids know their parents are upset. Parents don't need to worry about any negative effect. If parents are still *there* for their kids, although maybe a little less together than before, their kids will survive.

"Why did you have to get a divorce?"

On a day-to-day level, to counter the constant testing and pushing of your anxious kids, make things easier on yourself.

"Mom, do I have to take a bath tonight?"

I really shouldn't say this but tonight I just don't feel up to the hard time that I know he's going to give me.

"No."
"I don't?"
"No, you don't have to take a bath tonight. It's called postdivorce parent depression."
"It is?"
"Yes."
"Can you stay depressed? Can we do this for candy treats?"

LOSING A FAMILY

I'll always remember the time we went to a Red Sox game. Daddy got lost and had a fit. And then Mom had a fit because we were going to be late for the game. Then we couldn't get into the game because they were sold out, so we ended up going for a picnic in some park where there was this lady with two huge dogs. Dad told one of his stupid stories—the one about the three drunk bunny rabbits. Actually we had a real good time at the park, but on the ride home, Jennifer threw up.

Families are very special. A group of people with whom you have a special bond, with whom you feel totally intimate. A group of people who are always there, who are always yours, and with whom you share so many of the same experiences.

Then, divorce. If children never get to be part of that original family again, it is a loss. Yet if you ask children of divorced parents,

"Do you have a family?"

They will answer "yes."

And if you ask who's in your family?

They will usually include both of their parents.

"Me, Gregory, William, Mom, and Dad."

After a divorce, families remake and reshape themselves. If their parents are separated and divorced but both continue to play an ongoing role in their lives, if kids can count on them to be there and to have special times with them, kids will almost always include both parents as part of what they see as their family—even if their parents live apart. Or they will say they have two families. Divorce changes what the family is, but for most children divorce doesn't mean the end of *having* a family.

Sometimes the new constellation includes members such as grandparents, stepparents, or stepbrothers and stepsisters, but often the new family is just made up of who is left.

I'll always remember. Me, Jennifer, and Dad went to the Red Sox game. Except Dad got lost and we couldn't get in, and he had a big fit. So then he bought picnic stuff from a store and we had a picnic in this park that we found where there was a lady with two huge dogs. Dad made sandwiches. And then he told one of his stupid drunk bunny stories. We really did have a good time at the park, but Jennifer threw up on the way home.

RELATIVES

Greg's parents blamed me for the divorce and my relationship with them ended. Also, I heard from sources that they referred to me now as "the marriage wrecker" and worse. But Greg's parents have always liked the kids and the kids like them. The problem is that the kids used to see them during their time with Greg. But now that Greg's

*moved to Florida, it's up to me to deal with his parents if they're to
see the kids. And I'll be damned if I'm going to do Greg's parents
any favors, especially the way they've treated me since the divorce.*

People with whom you have a lifelong connection because
you're related are an absolute plus in a life. Some may be awful,
like constantly-critical-of-everything Aunt Louise or crude, insensitive cousin Philip. But, in general, relatives are people who care
about you and feel a connection to you that extends over a lifetime.
In a world in which making connections between people has become increasingly difficult, they are a built-in connectedness. Relatives are a nice thing to have.

With a divorce, however, members of your ex's side of the family
can turn into your enemies. However, this animosity usually does
not extend to your children.

"Fortunately, the children take after their father. They're lovely
kids—which is a wonder considering that *she* is their mother."

Often, these no longer friendly relatives are critical of you in
front of your kids. You might worry that such criticism will turn
your children against you, but this is a needless concern. The only
real risk is that too many such comments can turn the kids against
the relatives themselves.

"I don't like Grandma JJ because she always says bad stuff about
Mom."

Family is good. Extended family is good. Even if you don't like
them and they don't like you, they are a valuable piece of your
children's lives. Keeping these relationships going, despite the fact
that you may correctly feel that your ex's relatives deserve nothing
from you, that they treat you badly, maybe even bad-mouth you to
your kids, is a gift that you give your kids to make their lives nicer,
and perhaps even richer.

Anthony E. Wolf

DIVORCE'S EFFECT ON FUTURE ADULT RELATIONSHIPS

Doesn't our divorce give our kids a bad model of a marriage? Won't it affect their ability to maintain and trust relationships? Won't it affect their ability to stay in a marriage as an adult?

As I've discussed, one of the main psychological repercussions from a divorce is that the foundation of one's life—which was taken for granted—suddenly disappears. Now you see it—"Mom and Dad and me and Carrie"—and now you don't—"Mom. Dad. Me and Carrie."

This sudden loss can shake the foundations of trust, and trust is what you need in order to have meaningful relationships. So the following obvious question arises: Can I trust that as I go through life everything won't suddenly be pulled out from under me? Can I trust that people whom I love will always be there for me?

Yes. The truth is that what goes on between one's parents is not the greatest single factor in how well one forms future relationships in adult life. Yes, to most kids their parents' divorce is a betrayal. Yes, the model of parents who do not stay together gives kids future doubts about the permanence of marriage. But far more important, far and away the greatest influence on one's adult love relationships, is not what your parents did with each other, but how your parents, the people you loved the most as a kid, treated you. The love you receive in childhood builds the ability to love in return.

More than *anything* else, if I as a child have experienced a relationship with a parent where I am able to give love, have it happily received, and experience the joy of loving and being loved in return, divorce or not—I will seek out love as an adult.

5

Single Parenting

Maybe parenting was not so easy when you and your ex were still together. Maybe there were arguments over responsibility, over parenting style. Maybe your ex was such a bad parent that his or her absence from the home is a plus for you and your kids. Or maybe your ex was just a big kid, adding to, not helping with, the burden of parenting. Maybe. But having two parents in the home usually makes things easier. Being a single parent definitely has drawbacks.

"Mom, the bathtub's overflowing and Baby Winifred is out of her crib and I just threw up on the clean laundry."

One obvious hardship of single postdivorce parenting is that, as mentioned, there often is less money. Also, in most marriages, immediately following the split-up, there's less help with household work and child care.

He didn't help much. But he did help some.

What can get to be especially tough is that as a single parent you may go for long, uninterrupted stretches of time where it is only you and your kids. Taking care of them—hour after hour, day after day, week after week, maybe even month after month, without a break—can get pretty wearing.

It's just the kids and me. I love them. But sometimes, especially on weekends or school vacations, when it's just us for what can seem like endless chunks of time, I think I'm going to go crazy.

Parenting alone means that the full responsibility for all decisions about the kids, at least when they are with you, falls to you alone.

It used to be that when I had to decide something, there was this other person whom I could discuss it with. Should I force Melissa to take swimming lessons even though she doesn't want to? Should I send Scott to school when he complains of his stomachaches? Should I punish both of them for lying about what happened with the toaster? Even if Gary and I disagreed, at least the decision wasn't all my responsibility. Now it's every decision, all the decisions, and I feel like I'm completely alone. I know I'm not always right about everything and now if anything goes wrong the only person I can blame is myself.

Last, now that the children's other parent no longer shares a home with you, the one other person in the world who cares as much about and is as interested in your kids as you are is missing. The times together when you would take pride and joy in the experiences of your children—one of the true joys of parenting—are now gone.

"Barbara, look at what Jeffrey did," says his father, proudly displaying a piece of paper covered with crayon scribbles. "See how many colors he used this time."

"Why did you have to get a divorce?"

To anyone else in the world but Jeffrey's parents: Who cares?

"Yeah, that's great, Leo. It looks like paper with lots of scribbles on it. Your kid really is a genius."
"Well, he could be. See the use of color."
"Yeah, right. It's really good, Leo."

Others may be involved with your kids or may come into your life in different parenting roles, but usually there is no one quite like your children's other parent for really sharing what to you is special about your kids.

"Oh, you're right, Leo. Look, he even used turquoise."

What can a single parent do to compensate for the real hardship and isolation? The answer is that there is no way around some of this hardship, loneliness, and isolation. But at the same time, single parents can bring into their families a support team of as many other adults, relatives, and friends as possible. This support team should not be just people who might be potential backups in child care, or to whom you can turn in an emergency. You need to have a few people with whom you can simply talk about whatever you need to talk about. Just being able to share whatever you need or want to has great power in easing some of the burden.

"You would not believe my day. Justin and Jordan would not stop fighting. From the moment they woke up they were at each other. And then the burners on the stove suddenly go out. And I don't have a clue what I'm supposed to do. And then, like at the last possible moment, I remembered that I had to get Justin turtle food that he had promised to bring to school tomorrow. And I had to get both kids dressed again after I had just gotten them ready for bed, and back into the car, and them still fighting. The trip to Larry and Dave's Pet Food City was like a trip from hell."
"That sounds awful, Helena. You know, we don't go to Pet Food

City anymore after what happened that time I told you about with Keith and those dried pig's ears that they have."

Too Little Time

A conversation overheard at McDonald's between a mother who apparently works away from home a few nights a week and her approximately twelve-year-old son:

"Matt, I have a busy week. I'm only out in Plainview this week, which isn't that far, so that's good. Ron [the mother's boyfriend] can pick you up on Monday. And I think Karen [a friend] can get you on Tuesday. And I'll be home on Wednesday, so I can pick you up."
"At four," said Matt.
"No, I'll pick you up at day care at five-thirty."

And a conversation overheard at another McDonald's between a young single mother and another woman. The topic: holding down two jobs while trying to raise her kids:

"Often I only get to see them to say 'Hi' and 'Bye.'"

For some single parents, trying to keep a family afloat can create a situation where it seems like they hardly ever get to see their kids. It's a real worry for many single parents.

"But my mommy told me never to go anywhere with strangers."
"I *am* your mother, Todd."
"Cool."

It's not quite that bad for most parents, but many single parents have legitimate concerns about the amount of time they have for their kids. It's a difficult and persistent problem for single parents. They don't have enough time to work, to accomplish all the necessary day-to-day household chores, to get the kids where they need to be, and to do what they need to do, and still have any time left over to be a loving parent.

I worry that they just don't get enough of me. Kyle often asks, "Why do you have to work so much?" And I try to explain it to him, but I know he still wishes that he had more time with me. And then when I'm home, I'm always so busy. I just worry that they really are missing out. I worry that because they get so little time with me, it damages them.

Of course, this problem is not just reserved for single parents. In two-parent families with both parents working out of the home, time just to be with one's kids gets significantly squeezed. Still, it may not be as bad as it seems.

No, I am not saying that limited special time can substitute for quantities of just-plain-being-there-with-them time. But is there such a thing as quality time? Is there a kind of time that actually is a little more special, a little more nurturing? Maybe there is.

"Okay, it's eight-thirty."

"Is it time for our 'quality time'?"

"Yes, dear, it is. Come here and sit next to me on the couch. I'm going to tell you about my day. First I got up and then I woke you up. And then I went to the bathroom."

"Did you make a pee?"

"Yes, dear, I made a pee. Then I got dressed and I made breakfast."

"Your day is boring. Can I tell you about my day?"

"Yes, dear, whatever you want."

"My day was more interesting than your day."

"It probably was."

"You woke me up. And then I made a pee. And then I got dressed and then I had breakfast."

"Your day sounds a lot like my day."

"I know. But wait. My day gets better. After breakfast I went into the TV room and made pictures all over the walls with my Magic Markers."

"That's silly. You didn't do that."

"Yes, I did. My markers are invisible."

"No, they're not. That's silly."

"I know. And then I went to school. And this really happened. Trisha raised her hand in class and said she had to throw up. And Mrs. Kentler let her go to the bathroom. But I don't think she threw up."

"A lot of our stories seem to be about bathrooms."

"I know. Do you think people have meals in their bathrooms?"

"I don't know. That would be strange."

"Could we have a meal in the bathroom?"

"I don't think I would like that."

"I would."

"Well, dear, our quality time is over."

"It isn't very long, is it?"

"No, dear, it isn't."

"I wish it were longer."

"I know you do. But now I have to go in and do Tanya's quality time."

"I love you, Mommy."

"I love you, Kerry."

When I read this conversation out loud, the whole thing took slightly less than two minutes. I will guarantee that if a parent actually sits down and engages in this kind of conversation for just *two* minutes every day, he or she will be surprised to find out how much their kid cares about these two minutes and makes sure never to miss them. It's true, a little really does go a very long way.

"But it's only two minutes. How come you want it so much?"

"Because it's me and Mommy's 'quality time.' "

"But why is it so special?"
"It is. I don't know. It just is. It's me and Mommy."

Obviously, two minutes a day is not enough. But special time *is* special. A lot is better. But even a little of special just-you-and-them time touches a place deep inside kids. A little time where they get your full and undivided attention, where there is no purpose to the time, where nothing needs to be done or accomplished other than being together, is very powerful in the heads and hearts of children. More often than not, parents already provide it—usually at bedtime. But it can be anytime. Anytime it is just you and your kids. Sitting next to them while they are watching TV. Taking a little time to have them tell you about their day. Even just riding in the car, just the two of you. These little times add up. But you do want to make sure that they occur.

The time can be with more than one child, as long as the time is exclusively about you and them being together. However, some kids are very piggy about such time and will dominate, which you should notice and then make sure that each of your kids does get some full access to your time.

If this time is not given to each of your children, it needs to be.

But what makes a parent is not just time. Time is good, and when kids don't get enough parent time they do suffer. But what children care about above all else—what for them *is* a parent—is this adult whom they absolutely trust to love them above all others. It's as simple as that.

But I'm not sure that my kids do get to feel special. Most of the time if I'm paying attention to them, it's always about correcting them or getting them to do stuff. I don't know if they do get to feel special. Mainly I yell at them.

Kids can handle getting yelled at by a parent. Especially if it is by a parent whose love they're certain of. But if that is all they get, this is a problem.

But there's so much that I need to get them to do, so many times I have to correct their behavior. What am I supposed to do?

The answer is simple: If all you ever have time for is what has to be done, then maybe some of the things that have to be done *don't* have to be done. Much of being an effective parent—single or otherwise—comes down to making difficult choices. If this means that some things *don't* get done, then maybe that has to happen. Maybe accomplishing everything is asking too much in these times.

Should I really try to get them to keep their rooms picked up? How much do I care about table manners? If the kids are yelling at each other, but not causing harm, do I even want to intervene? Should I give up on the kids not making food messes on the couch when they're watching TV? Should I cancel Dawn's tap dancing lessons—at least for the rest of the year—because Wednesdays are getting too difficult?

Some choices are hard. But if you have kids, one choice must be that there is some time for just you and them. But, again, time is not what makes a parent. Absolute and unconditional love makes a parent. This love is what they carry with them every minute of the day, for the rest of their lives.

DO KIDS NEED A SAME-SEX PARENT?

"How is it that boys act, Mommy? I keep forgetting. Do I like Barbies or Xtro Action Men?"

Maybe this is an exaggeration, but single parents do worry about their children's not having a role model of the same sex.

I worry for Richard. Since his father left, Richard rarely gets to see him. At home it's just me and his sister, and sometimes my mother when she babysits. He hardly has any men in his life. I worry that he's growing up without really knowing a man. With no man as a role model.

It's a normal and reasonable concern. How will children, without the daily in-the-home model of the same-sex parent, learn a clear sense of their own gender identity? The fact is they do. Maybe some of this identity is innate—biological programming that dictates certain kinds of behavioral tendencies. Certainly much of the sex-role modeling children get—whether they have a same-sex parent in the home or not—is from the world around them, which is not lacking in role models. They also have role models in other children of the same gender, in the stories they're told, in books and TV and movies, and in other adults of the same sex. Children also learn gender roles from what the time and the culture say those roles are supposed to be. The news just seeps in through every pore of their bodies.

The advantage of having a same-sex parent as a role model really depends on whether that parent is a *good* role model. Not all are.

"Esther, where the hell's my beer? Roger, your mother is clueless."

Cool. I'm going to grow up like Daddy. I'm going to make funny jokes while I put down women.

Parents who display positive and healthy behaviors of their sex, whose behavior may even serve as a contrast to some of the not so healthy stereotypes, can be a powerful influence.

Mommy cares about how she looks, and she helps me to look nice. But she never seems to go crazy about her weight. She seems to take a lot of pride in what she's done in her life. She cares about how she looks, but I can see that for her it isn't everything.

The bottom line about same-sex parents as role models is simply not about a child learning how to fit into his or her sex-role type. Society at large provides more than enough of that—if anything too much emphasizing of set roles for each sex.

"Mom, do I have to watch football games?"
"Hush, Clifford, don't you want to have friends?"

"Mom, do I have to keep reading these magazines about how to be thin and cute?"
"Hush, Mary Ellen, don't you want to have friends?"

The bottom line is whether or not a child gets to experience a parent of each gender who can model all the good characteristics of being an adult. A mother who is both strong and compassionate. A father who is both strong and compassionate. And if a child gets two like that he is lucky. Many kids—not of divorced parents—do not get two such parents. Some do not get one. What should a parent do whose child has little or no contact with a same-sex parent? Be the best possible role model of a caring adult. It is enough.

6

When the Other Parent Is a Problem

Even though you are divorced, your kids still have this *other* parent about whom they care intensely and who also has a significant influence in their lives. You may have gotten a divorce, but you are still stuck with your ex as a major part of your life—for better or for worse. Often, it may seem for worse.

WHEN THEY DRIFT AWAY

Jennifer was seven and Ricky was five when their parents, Carl and Maria, separated. Up until the time of the separation, Jennifer and Ricky's dad had been a big part of their lives. He was involved in much of the child raising and had a loving and close relationship with both children. But his relationship with their mother had been rocky from the start. Finally, following a particularly nasty fight, Carl moved out and temporarily moved in with his parents, who lived about half an hour away. A year later the divorce was official.

According to the divorce settlement, Carl would see the children on weekends and at least one night a week. In the beginning, he saw Jennifer and Ricky often. He even thought that maybe when he got settled in a place of his own, he might try to get custody.

However, because of the distance he now lived from his children and the extra hours he was taking on at work, he found it increasingly hard to fit in time to see them. Then he met Laura. She had two kids of her own and lived in the opposite direction from where his kids lived. More and more he found himself canceling his time with Jennifer and Ricky, leaving his ex-wife infuriated and his kids disappointed.

Within two years of when Carl and I separated, he hardly saw Jennifer and Rick at all. I was always stuck having to answer for him to them.

"Mom, why can't we see Dad anymore?"

"Mom, when are we going to get to see Dad? I miss him."

And sometimes Rick would actually cry at night,

"Dad doesn't like us, does he, Mom? He likes Laura, Casey, and Andrea better, doesn't he?"

What could I say? I thought that was exactly what was going on. It was always some excuse or another, and Jennifer, who is sharp, would notice other things.

"I don't think Laura wants Dad to like us. I think she wants him just for herself and her kids."

It's just not fair to them. They love him and they feel rejected by him. Jennifer doesn't cry about it the way Rick will sometimes, but I think it breaks both of their hearts. I could hardly believe that he could do this to them—except that I know the kind of man he is— but when we were married, he really was close to them.

I've told them to say to him that they would like to see him more. But they're afraid he'll get mad. Actually Rick did ask his father a couple of times whether he might see them more often, but their dad just made excuses.

I've talked to him. I told him how Rick cries at night. I've talked to my lawyer, who said the bottom line is that there is no real leverage to force their father to see Rick and Jennifer if he doesn't want to. I've written him letters. I can't stand what it's doing to the kids.

"Why did you have to get a divorce?"

Sometimes after I confront him, he'll see the kids a couple of weeks in a row and they're so happy. But then the visits drop off again and Rick's heart is broken all over again. Jennifer doesn't get as upset—actually she's beginning to sour a bit on her dad. You can't blame her.

I don't know what to do to make their dad understand, to get him to pay more regular attention to his kids. It's a crime. It really is.

This is not an uncommon story of how a parent, usually a father, even one who had been involved with his kids, gradually fades away after a divorce, maybe to the point of having very little contact with them at all.

Sometimes they lose contact because of a move to a distant place.

"After him and Mom got divorced, Dad left Chicago and moved to Florida. I was supposed to go to visit him every summer, but I only went once. Now I talk to him when he calls on Christmas and my birthday—if he remembers."

Even if the distance involved in a move is not so great, it often happens that, little by little, the other parent nevertheless slips out of the children's lives.

"Yeah, my dad lives over in Crestville. It's not far, but I hardly ever see him. He'll call, like on holidays, but that's about it. Last time I saw him was—I don't know—maybe a year ago."

"Do you care?"

"I used to. But now I really don't think about him much one way or the other."

"Do you like him?"

"I used to think he was a jerk for always disappointing me. But now, like I said, I don't really think about him."

Or perhaps:

"I think he's a jerk. I hate him. If you have kids you can't just desert them. But really I don't care that much anymore. I haven't seen or talked to him in three years. He wasn't interested in me, I'm not interested in him."

Sometimes a new partner's influence makes it difficult for the absent parent to maintain a relationship with the "old" family.

Since Beth married the children's father, she's done everything she could to have it be her and her kids. She's done her best to exclude Casey and Tracy from their life. And she's done a good job. He never seems to have time for them anymore. Everything's about their family. It's like James and the twins are his real children and Casey and Tracy are I don't know what. He's forgotten his own kids.

The absence of the ex can be very hard on the parent who's left to raise the kids and witness the loss and heartache. Yet there is a cold truth about such situations. If visits begin to be a burden for the absentee parent, something they feel they *should* do but really don't feel like doing—when push comes to shove, it's not going to happen.

Parents stay involved for the long haul with their kids only for one reason. They want to. And if, for whatever reason, visits start to become more of a burden than a pleasure, they start to fall off.

I don't know. I know I should go see the kids today. I mean, I do want to see them. I like them. They're good kids. Though Jennifer has been a little cold to me lately. But Laura's been after me to do the lawn and I just don't see how I can do everything today without it all being a big hassle. And besides, this is supposed to be my day off.

It does no good to try to defend your ex's absence.

Dad's New Family

"Your dad loves you and Tracy. It's just that he gets very busy. He loves you. He should find the time for you, but he doesn't."

That only invalidates their feelings and says you don't understand.

If Dad loves me, how come he never sees me and spends so much more time with Beth's kids? I don't get it.

It's much better to be honest.

"Dad doesn't really love us that much, does he? He likes Beth and her kids better than us, doesn't he?"

"I don't know what's in your dad's head. But you're right. He sure doesn't seem to pay much attention to Tracy and you."

Much better is this honesty—painful as it may be—so they can come to terms with the reality. Your seemingly harmless dishonesty will only support a fiction that in the end can only drag out their futile hopes.

Well, Mom says Dad loves me. Maybe we'll get to have more time with him. Maybe they're just very busy like Mom says. I don't know, though. He sure must be very busy.

The truth is much better because, after all, it is reality.

Dad likes his new family better. He deserted us. We're his kids and he deserted us.

Attempts to push for more involvement from a disinterested parent do nobody any good either, though he or she may briefly respond to the pressure.

Yeah, I guess Maria is right. I'll try to see the kids more often.

But then the visits invariably drop off once again.

In this case you become complicit in prolonging an agonizing process that probably has already gone on too long, because, ironically, this period of rejection is also a period of hope. Anyone who has been on the wrong side of an adult relationship that's ending knows how hope can drag on endlessly if the rejecting party holds out the slightest reason to hope.

"Well, he wouldn't have called to wish me happy birthday if he didn't still care about me. His birthday's coming up. Maybe I'll buy him some nice jewelry."

Kids hold on to the same kind of hope.

"Mommy, do you think Daddy will take us this weekend?"
"I don't know dear, it's been a while."
"But he could, couldn't he? It could happen. Daddy could take us. And we'd have a good time. It could happen."

The final end to the relationship can take months or it can take years. Visits grow fewer and fewer, more and more plans are canceled at the last minute or simply skipped with no explanation. Finally, it gets to the point where that parent is no longer a meaningful part of a child's life, which is a major loss, but at least there is an end. The loss becomes clear and now one can try to get over it. If it's going to end, it's kinder not to drag it out longer than its natural course. As hard as it may be to watch, bear in mind that defending your ex or pushing him or her to be more involved is not doing your kids any favors.

WHEN YOUR EX TELLS YOU WHAT TO DO—YOUR RIGHTS

Although some parents do remain on good terms following a divorce, they did not get a divorce for nothing. Therefore, a more common problem regarding the other parent is not that they disappear, but that they don't.

"Karen, Stephen's exhausted when I pick him up for the weekend. He tells me you let Marianne and him stay up until nine on school nights. I think it's too late for Marianne, but it's definitely too late for Stephen. I don't know what you can be thinking. I'm sure it's affecting him in school and I worry about his health."

The good news about divorce is that when you are with your kids, your ex can't tell you what to do. For better or for worse, when you are with your children, you are the sole person in charge.

Your ex can *say* all he or she wants, but unless you are certifiably abusing or neglecting your children, your ex has no control over what goes on. In actual practice, unless there is proven abuse or neglect, courts almost always back the principle that what parents do when they're with the children is their business and nobody else's. Which leads to a major fact about being a divorced parent: *When you're with your kids, nobody can tell you what to do.*

"Candace, the girls tell me that all they ever do each day after school is sit around, talk on the phone, and watch movies. How can that be good for them? They're turning into vegetables. You're their mother. You need to get them to be more active."

Perhaps the girls' father is right. Maybe the girls' mother should restrict their phone use and movie watching in the afternoon, get the girls to be more active. But maybe the girls and their mother are quite content with what they are doing, and maybe the girls are doing just fine. Either way, their mother doesn't have to change what she does when she is with her daughters. Hence:

"Gosh, Roger, I'm sorry you're not happy with what I do with the girls, but I'm content with what I'm doing."
"Well, it's no good for the girls, sitting around all the time watching TV. Besides, I see what's on in the afternoons. It's all stupid. And Valerie is putting on weight. I can see it."

The best response to such criticism is to reiterate your comfort and confidence in your parenting.

"I'm sorry you feel that way, but I'm content with what I'm doing with the kids."
"You should have more consideration for their needs. You're creating kids who are growing up to be blobs."
"Gosh, I don't know what to say to you, Roger."

It's also a nicer way of saying, "Stay the hell out of my business with the kids, and there's nothing you can do about it even if you want to."

Trying to defend yourself rarely leads to anything positive. In the earlier scenario with Stephen and Marianne, their mother, Karen, might have responded defensively to their father's phone call:

"Hello, Karen. It's me, Arnold."

"Yes, I know."

"You don't have to get sarcastic with me."

"I wasn't getting sarcastic with you. What do you want?"

"The children have been telling me how at your house during the week, they get to stay up until nine watching TV. I just worry, especially with Stephen. I don't think that gives him enough sleep. Sometimes he complains about being tired during the day at school."

"I think Stephen gets all the sleep he needs when he is with me."

"Well, all I know is that when he is at my house and stays up that late on weekends, if we ever have to go somewhere the next day early, he's totally zonked. I know he wants to stay up late, but it could be affecting his work in school."

"I'm not getting reports from school of his falling asleep."

"That's not the point. It could be affecting his work, his concentration."

"Arnold, I do not think there is a problem."

"You don't know if there's a problem. You just give in all the time to whatever he wants, because it's too much effort to stand up to him."

"And I suppose you're Mr. Perfect about parenting?"

"At least I put what's best for my kids first."

"You never put anybody but yourself first."

The conversation went downhill from there.

If Stephen's mother wants to discuss his bedtime at her house with his father, she can. But it is her choice. If she does not wish to discuss the subject, nothing says that she has to. In regard to such decisions, Stephen's mother is not answerable to his father nor does she have to defend herself. If she is comfortable with what she is doing, all she has to say is:

"The children have been telling me how at your house during the week, they get to stay up until nine watching TV. I just worry, especially with Stephen. I don't think that gives him enough sleep. Sometimes he complains about being tired during the day at school."

"I'm sorry you feel that way. But I am comfortable with what I am doing."

"But that's the problem. You do what you're comfortable with, not what's best for the kids."

"I'm sorry you feel that way. But I am comfortable with what I am doing. Is there anything else you want to speak to me about, Arnold?"

"That's what you always do. You never want to hear about anything that's necessary for the kids."

"I don't think this conversation is going anywhere productive. I'll speak to you at another time. Goodbye, Arnold."

You're the boss.

Of course, the reverse is true: When the kids are with Arnold, he's the boss.

"Mom, Dad keeps telling me to stop my sniffing and you know I can't control it. And I tried to explain but he yelled at me and said that I whined all the time and was going to turn out to be a hypochondriac, just like you. And I got so upset I couldn't eat supper and then he yelled at me about that. But I couldn't help it and I didn't know what to do."

When I married him I simply didn't understand the kind of person he was. But I certainly found out. He never understood about kids. He has no patience with them. I don't even think he likes them. I think he sees the kids because his parents tell him to. He'll say things to the kids that parents just shouldn't say to their children. Sometimes he'll be cruel with them. And he hasn't a clue that that's not what you're supposed to be doing with kids.

I worry when they're with him. What's going to happen? What's he going to do? And I feel bad for the kids. I worry for them.

Maybe he is too harsh. Maybe he does pay little or no attention to the kids when they're with him. Maybe he has little or no control. Perhaps he's well-meaning but shows consistently poor parenting judgment. But the hard fact is: What holds true for your time with your kids holds true for your ex's time with them. All you can do is stand by and watch. Unless there is actual abuse or neglect, you have no say over what goes on when your kids are with him, unless he grants it.

INTERVENING TO CHANGE YOUR EX

If you couldn't change your ex when the two of you were married, what chance do you have now that you're divorced? You're not wrong to try. Sometimes your words might sink in, but it's not likely. It can be very frustrating.

"Dad, Mom isn't letting me watch *Jamie's Family*. You know it's my favorite program. But since it switched times, it only comes on when I'm at her house."

It is Jeremy's favorite program. He really loves it. He looks forward to it every week. I wish his mother could be a little more sensitive, a little less inflexible. I know it's stupid but he really does love the show.

What any divorced parent would like to be able to do is to communicate to an ex that maybe a little more sensitivity, a little more flexibility, would make a real difference for your child. Unfortunately, all too often such interventions produce little good.

"Hello, Ruth."

"What?"

"It's me, Harry."

"What do you want?"

"Jeremy says you won't let him watch *Jamie's Family*. It really is his favorite program."

"Harry, he has you wrapped around his little finger."

"It *is* his favorite program. It's only once a week and Jeremy really does look forward to it. He gets so disappointed when he misses it."

"The program's on when we eat supper at my house. I suppose he didn't tell you that."

"Couldn't you be a little more flexible—for him? He really does care about the program."

"You're going to tell me when to eat supper? You're something else."

"I'm not telling you when to eat supper. I'm just . . ."

"Then what do you call what you're doing? You can't run things over here, Harry. I know you'd like to."

"I'm not trying to run things, Ruth. Can't we ever talk about what's best for Jeremy?"

"You're not interested in what's best, you just want to run things over here too."

"You really are impossible to talk to. I can't deal with you, Ruth."

"Good. Then let's hang up." Click.

There is another problem with interventions. Though obviously your point is to help your kids, interventions may inadvertently turn out to be to your kids' disadvantage.

"Mom, I don't think Dad likes me. He yells at me all the time. I was playing with my fork and dropped it on the floor, and he got really mad and really yelled at me. He always yells at me about everything."

And Philip started to cry.

"Your father makes me so mad. I don't know what his problem is. If it's any consolation, as you know, he yelled at me all the time too. He's a very difficult man, Philip."

Whether you are divorced or still married, the issue remains the same. It's very hard to stand by and watch another parent behave toward your children in a way you know is painful for them.

I suffer for Philip. I do. I can't stand to hear how his father treats him. Philip gets so upset.

Philip's mother, once again seething at his bad treatment at the hands of his father, called her ex-husband to tell him how much he had upset Philip and how he should not always be yelling at him. Yet any interventions on her part can teach a bad lesson. In this situation, Philip learns that if he has trouble with his father, he can always turn to his mother. She not only understands him but also, as he has learned, will always intervene for him. The risk is that Philip will simply bypass the relationship with his father and not learn to work out anything with him. In effect, during his time with his father, he will hold his breath until he gets back home to his mother. He will simply suffer silently and take his suffering to his mother, who does understand.

Mom loves me. I'll get her to deal with Dad.

If this goes on for a long time, Philip probably never learns to cope with his father. Also, his mother doesn't want some of Philip's bond with her to be based on his bad relationship with his father.

"Did Mommy's treasure have a bad time with his nasty father?"
"Oh, I did, Mommy, I did."
"And does Mommy's treasure want to tell Mommy all about the bad time so that he can feel better?"
"Oh, I do, Mommy, I do."
"And isn't it nice here with Mommy, who always understands?"
"Oh, it is, Mommy, it is."

It would be much better if Philip were left to deal with his father on his own. Though there may be times that will be hard, eventually Philip will most likely learn to cope with his father.

"Dad's a jerk. And he yells at me a lot. And I don't particularly even like him. But I can deal with him."

Maybe over time Philip and his dad will even develop a relationship. Which is why the greater wisdom is—usually—to stay out of it. Be understanding, but trying to change things "over there" rarely gets anyone anywhere.

"I don't exactly love Dad, but I can deal with him. And I think he respects me. I do feel good about the relationship. Dad gets me mad, but I can handle it. And I know that down deep he likes me, even though sometimes he really can be a total jerk."

Again, the greater wisdom is to stay out of these situations. You can support and sympathize, but not too much. Listen and understand, but not much more.

"I know you hate it when your dad yells at you."
"I do. He yells all the time."
"It's hard sometimes."
"It is. He's a jerk."

If the bad times at the other parent's really are too unpleasant, if they really are too bad, too much for the Philips of the world to handle, then, yes, all interventions and commiserations are appropriate to protect them. But if the situation is less traumatic than that, parents want to be careful so that well-meant but unnecessary protection does not end up short-circuiting any chance of a relationship. In the end, you need to let your children play out their relationship with their other parent—for better or for worse—on their own.

Shut Out of Part of Their Lives

A corollary to your and your ex's not having any control over each other's parenting is that you often don't even know what is going on.

"How was it at your dad's?"
"Okay."
"What did you do?"
"Not too much. You know, regular stuff."

It drives me crazy. When they come back from being with their father, it's like there's a wall of silence. I really don't know what goes on when they are with him. Sometimes I'll get snatches of information. But mainly they say little. I think he tells them not to talk about what happens when they're with him. I mean, I know he doesn't abuse them or anything, but I find it very hard to deal with. They're my kids and there's a part of them that's not mine at all.

A part of your children's lives is not part of your life. You have absolutely no control over this other part of their lives and often may not even know what goes on when they are with your ex. It's hard and can be one of the major losses for a parent in a divorce. After all, it was not part of the deal when you and your ex decided to have children.

WHEN YOUR EX IS A BAD INFLUENCE

It can be hard not knowing everything that goes on. But often it can be harder when you do know.

You don't know him like I do. You don't know the kind of person he is. The idea that the kids will grow up and spend time with him, looking up to him as their father, I really worry about it. His values, the way he looks at life. I dread that any of that would become part of them.

"Ooh, Dad's so cool, Mom. He has this friend Maxie who has really long hair and rides a huge Harley and he tells the coolest stories about the three times he was in jail."

You legitimately worry that there is this other person whom your kids like and care about, with whom they spend a significant amount of time, over whom you have basically zero control, and who in your opinion is not a good person at all and will influence your kids to go in bad ways too. However, the fact remains that unless there is clear evidence of abuse, the courts today almost always support your ex's right to see the children. Besides, bad character traits are very hard to prove and are just about never successful grounds for limiting a child's time with a given parent.

"Your honor, here are pictures showing that the children's father violated the court order stating that Maxie 'The Hook' Detweiler

Having No Control When They are with Your Ex Can Be Tough

—convicted three times for drug dealing—was not to be at his house when the children were there."

"She's lying, your honor. She took those pictures last July before the court order. She's just looking for anything, like she always does, so she can get back at me for leaving her. She's crazy, your honor."

The possible warping influence on your kids by your ex—especially a noncustodial ex who you think is a bad role model parent—is more of a worry than a reality. The actual influence that the other parent has over your children has mainly to do with how well or badly that parent treats them, rather than the kind of person that parent is. Liking the other parent doesn't mean that kids buy the rest of the package. Although the bad parent's influence is definitely there, it doesn't negate a parent's love and caring, which is what matters to children.

No parent can completely shape who his or her child is or becomes. Whether they have an evil other parent or not, the temptations and opportunities to do ill are not lacking in the life of any child. You cannot fully protect them from the world they live in. You cannot protect them from bad friends, bad TV, bad other parents. You can only do your best in your time with your kids and hope that in the face of all that the world will throw at them, what you have done will be enough. Fortunately, it usually is.

Provided the other parent is not abusive, letting them have a relationship with that parent may be a risk but it is a risk worth taking. It's simply better to have two parents than one. Why? Because two is more. No matter how wonderful one parent may be, having a second parent provides another person with whom a child can have a relationship that is deep, caring, and intimate. And because everyone is different, that relationship will be different. Not better, but different, and children are enriched by it. It can be hard to let go—to stay out of or not get in the way of that relationship. Yet if you do allow it to happen, your children will gain something of real value in their lives. Consider it a gift to your children.

IF YOU THINK THERE IS ABUSE

The exception to all that has been said in this chapter is that if you suspect that there is neglect or abuse, you must do everything you can in order to prevent the contact. It's not your role to determine with certainty whether abuse or neglect is actually taking place. Your responsibility is to report it to the local child-abuse authorities, usually the local Department of Social Services. If you are unsure whom to contact, call the police, a local hospital, or a local pediatrician and ask whom to call to report it.

Obviously, reporting the suspicion of child neglect or abuse is not something to undertake lightly, and there can be serious repercussions from such a report. But if you genuinely suspect that your child is being abused or neglected by his or her other parent, that concern must outweigh all others. Besides the real risk to their safety, child abuse is devastating to children's psychological well-being and must be stopped. An investigation by authorities may not be able to substantiate any abuse. However, often when there is no finding of abuse, the accusation serves as a warning. And when warned, the accused hears it.

But what if there is mental abuse? Like how his father is constantly calling him a "little jerk" or a "loser," which Andrew tells me his father does and I believe him. I know it's not like physical abuse but I still think it's hurting him.

Because children cannot help having a strong attachment to their other parent and care very much about how that other parent treats them and makes them feel, they have a problem if that other parent treats them badly. Most devastating about having a parent who treats a child badly is the effect on the child's self-perception and self-esteem.

Dad treats me like I'm a jerk and a loser. So I guess I'm a jerk and a loser.

If you genuinely feel that what is going on between the other parent and your kids is bad for them and damaging—even if not certifiable abuse—then you want to do all that you can do to prevent it from continuing. You can try talking to the other parent. But, as often is the case, if direct intervention by you is hopeless or meets with no success, then you may have to try legal channels. Sometimes going through lawyers and courts in order to eliminate situations or behaviors that are psychologically damaging to one's kids may work out satisfactorily. However, the famous "psychological abuse" is so hard to prove that it virtually never can be used as real leverage by one parent against the other. Often, the use of legal means merely ends up quite frustrating, with little change occurring. Still, if you genuinely believe that what is going on is significantly damaging to your kids, and if your direct intervention has failed to change anything, for their benefit and your peace of mind, pursue the legal channels.

Fortunately, even when kids have a significantly negative experience at the hands of another parent, they have damage insurance: you. If children have one good, strong, consistently present parent throughout their childhood, they have a built-in powerful and important defense: they have no need for the other, more negative parent. Furthermore, if children are ever to rise above the experience of having a bad parent, somewhere along the line they must take an extraordinarily important step—they must reject the bad parent. This ever so important step becomes so much easier and so much more possible for a child if he has in place a solid, dependable relationship that says he's basically a good kid.

Gosh, with Mom I don't feel like a jerk and a loser. I feel that I'm just fine. Somebody's bad. But maybe it's not me. Maybe I'm not a jerk and a loser at all. Maybe it's him. Maybe he's a mean, bad man. I don't know what his problem is, but I'm not the one with the problem. He is.

7

Kids Caught in the Middle

At a cousin's wedding reception both of Kenneth's now divorced parents were in attendance.

"Hey, big Mr. K, sit over here with your old man. I've been saving a place for you."

"Kenny, sweetheart, I'm over here," called his mother. "I've saved a place for you right next to Mommy."

Perplexed, Kenneth looked back and forth between his two beckoning parents.

"Don't listen to her, champ. Your place is next to me."

Kenneth started moving toward where his father was sitting.

"Sit with your father and you break my heart," called out his mother.

Kenneth edged back in the direction of his mother.

"This is what you do to your old man after all I've done for you?"

Kenneth hesitated, motionless. But then he swiftly ran to the door of a side room, opened it, went in, and closed the door. Immediately the door reopened and two identical Kenneths emerged—Kenneth and his clone that he had had made a month before and which had been delivered only just before the wedding.

"Coming, Dad," called one of the Kenneths. "This is great. You and me, Dad. Forget Mom."

"That's my boy," said Kenneth's proud father.

"I'll sit next to you, Mommy," said the other Kenneth. "Why would I ever want to sit with my stupid father?"

"That's my guy," said Kenneth's happy mother.

Unfortunately the above is not an option currently available to children of divorced parents.

I Like Them Both the Same

"Whom do you like better, your mother or your father?"

"I like them the same."

"Well, don't you maybe like one of them the teeniest bit better than the other?"

"No, I like them both the same. Exactly the same."

"What would happen if you did like one of your parents better than the other?"

"But I don't."

"But let's just say you did."

"But I don't."

"Well, what would happen to some other kid whose parents were divorced and he liked one of his parents better than the other?"

"The parent he didn't like best wouldn't like him."

"What would they do?"

"They wouldn't love him anymore."

Kids have to think this way. As they see it, a preference for one or the other parent is just too great a risk. They could lose a parent's love, and just thinking about that possibility is far too scary.

I hate it when they say stuff about each other. I hate it when they ask me questions. I just want to be able to have a nice time. I'm always afraid if I say something wrong, they'll be mad at me.

Parents understand this, at least implicitly, and most parents do their best to keep their children out of parental arguments, not to ask them to make judgments or choose sides.

Yet parents pull their kids into their parental disputes all the time. In fact, what's to stop a parent from saying all kinds of stuff? Nothing. What's to stop him or her from distorting the truth and feeding the kids a completely warped picture of everything? Nothing.

"Mommy said to tell you that you are a selfish bastard for not paying for me to get a new pair of sneakers."

"Daddy says that the reason you didn't get the child support check was because his business was very slow last month and he couldn't afford it."

"Mom, Dad says the divorce was your fault because you had sex with Willie Hapgood."

What can be said or done in response to any of these statements without putting the kids in the middle? Very little. What can be done without hurting them? Very little. Can you regularly tell your side without making things worse for your children? The truth is that you cannot. But it is totally normal and in no way whatsoever wrong or pathological to feel the *need* to set the record straight with your kids when your ex doesn't play by the rules. It's impossible not to, really, if you're a normal human being.

Why? Because the unfairness can be pretty hard to take, because you assume your children are thinking ill of you if you don't. We cannot stand that our kids should judge us badly even if often the issues are complicated, having to do with adult matters they really can't understand anyway.

Mommy's okay. I mean, I love Mommy and all. But it was her fault that they got divorced. And Daddy's right. He tries to be rea-

sonable, but she acts immature about anything that has to do with Daddy. Actually I feel sorry for Mommy.

No way could any parent remotely tolerate the idea that their kids would ever think the above.

So with an ex who doesn't play by the rules, who pulls your kids into disputes, and with your need to counter, what can you do that won't put or keep your kids in the middle? You simply refuse to play that game. Most of the time this solution works, and works well, as you'll see in the rest of this chapter. When your ex tries to bring your kids into the middle, you take them out of it. Kids are only caught in the middle if both parents participate—it's only a contest if both are contesting.

When Kids Take Sides

Kids don't want to take sides. They want their relationship with each parent to be as free as possible from any concerns that have to do with the other parent. They have no desire to be caught in the middle between two feuding parents.

I don't want to have to worry about any of that stuff. I just don't want to. When I'm at Dad's I want to be able to be with him the way I want to, and I don't want to have to worry about what Mom will think, and the same when I'm with Mom. I don't want to have to think about any of that other stuff. It just screws things up. I just want to be able to have a nice time with each of them. That's what I want.

If kids *do* find themselves in the middle of a conflict and then actually side with one parent or the other, it's usually because they perceive that one or the other wants them to, that it is, in fact, a condition of staying in good favor with that parent.

Jennifer to her father:

Joys of Being in the Middle

"It's not right that Vivian [her father's girlfriend] and her kids are always there whenever I come to see you. It should just be you and me."

Maybe this is how Jennifer truly felt, but in this particular case maybe it was not. Maybe Jennifer had actually liked it with Vivian and the kids there. Maybe it was definitely more fun than with just her often boring father. And maybe Jennifer had gotten a very definite message from her mother.

"What? Vivian and those two kids were there again? Your father has a lot of nerve. You're his child. He can't take time away from Vivian and those kids to spend it alone with his only daughter? I feel very sorry for you, Jennifer."

Jennifer had clearly heard her mother's outrage at her father for now having a girlfriend. She had also heard that if she wanted to stay in her mother's good graces, she would do well to echo her mother's feelings. Jennifer took sides, but it really wasn't her own doing.

PROTECTING THE OTHER PARENT

"You've got to face it, Kyle, your father is a sleazy, unreliable bum."
"No, he isn't. He's not. You shut up about Dad!"

Let's say that Kyle's father *is* a sleazy, unreliable bum and that Kyle well knows it. Regardless, most kids do not want to hear about it—especially from their other parent.

Mom always says bad stuff about Dad. And maybe I sort of know it's true. But I love Dad. And I want him to love me, so I don't care about all the bad stuff she says about him. Even if it's true. Actually I wish she wouldn't say any of it, because I'm going to love Dad no matter what she says. And all her saying that stuff does is make me feel that she wants me to not like him. And I don't want to get her mad at me either. I want her to love me too. I just wish she wouldn't say any of that stuff.

Criticism paints the other parent in a tarnished light, makes that parent less perfect, and, if children buy into the criticism, gets in the way of their ability to love that parent as much as they would like. Most kids do not want to hear one parent disparaging the other. They consider it an attack against something they want to like. So they'll try to hear no evil.

I love Mommy and Daddy both. And I want them to love me. And I don't want to think bad things about them.

You may fear that they are not facing the reality about their other parent. But far more often than not they know the reality only too well. And it makes them sad. The last thing they want is to hear about it from you.

USING YOUR KIDS AS A MOUTHPIECE

Henry to his mother:
"Mom, Dad says you're not careful about our health. He says you haven't been dressing Terrance warm enough, which is why he got a cold."

The most normal response might be:

"I don't know what your father's talking about. I dress Terrance just fine."

This would seem like a perfectly good response, and it's certainly a completely normal response, except that it puts the mother in the position of defending herself against the father's accusation. Still, it's preferable to an all-out counterattack, which serves only to pull the kids deeper into the battle.

"Your father should mind his own business. Who does he think he is, telling me how to dress the two of you?"

Or even worse, because it asks the children to actively participate in the battle:

"Tell your father that I dress the two of you just fine. And that if he has a problem with that he can tell me directly."

"Mom says she dresses us fine. And that if you have a problem you should call her."
"She does, does she? Well, I'll give her a call."

Nor should the children's mother call their father to tell him that he should deliver the messages himself.

"Henry said that you said that I don't dress Terrance warmly enough. If you have a problem, I would appreciate your talking to me directly—not going through the children."

This response is perhaps okay the *first* time the children were used as a mouthpiece. But they've probably been used many times before. In any case, calling their father has served mainly to continue the battle. For Henry, the call meant that his relaying the message was the trigger for yet another fight between his parents.

If I hadn't told Mom then she wouldn't have called Dad and yelled at him. But then Dad would have been mad at me for not giving the message to Mom. Or I could have lied to Dad and said I told Mom, but I don't like lying to Dad. Besides, sometimes he finds out and then he's really mad.

Best, because it doesn't continue the battle and takes the children right out of it, would be:

"Mom, Dad says you're not careful about our health. He says you haven't been dressing Terrance warm enough, which is why he got a cold."
"I'm sorry your father feels that way, but I am comfortable with how I dress the two of you."

"Why did you have to get a divorce?"

Unspoken:

Your father can say whatever he wants, but I decide what happens when the two of you are with me.

And that's it. Nothing more. And if they still want to continue:

"But Dad says you don't dress us warm enough. We should dress warmer."

The answer is always the same:

"When you are with me, I decide what I think is best."

Your statement emphasizes that when they are with you, you are the boss of what goes on. It says that what they relay from their father is not going to change anything one way or the other. It gives them the message that when they are with you they simply do not have to worry about issues between you and their other parent. You will not get into it. They can relay messages or not. It makes no difference.

And if they were delivering the message because they felt—as is most often the case—that they needed to in order to stay in the good graces of their other parent, they have done their duty by their father.

"Did you tell your mom?"
"Yes."
"What did she say?"
"She said she was sorry you felt that way, but when we're with her she decides."
"Your mother has no concern for your and Terrance's health. I really worry for the two of you."

But Henry doesn't worry about it. He's off the hook and relieved. He did his duty by his father in delivering the message and reporting her reply. It's not his fault that his mother says what she does, and his father will not blame him. Since his mother doesn't seem to care, Henry is not caught in the middle. Because his mother is simply not playing the game, there are not two fighting parents to get caught between.

It is like a court trial in which your ex is the complainant, you the defendant, and your kids both prosecuting attorney and judge.

"The defendant," says Henry, "is accused of child neglect, not dressing her child warmly enough. What has the defendant to say in her defense?"

"I'm not playing. The prosecuting attorney will please try not to track mud into the kitchen, but he might also like a cookie and some cider."

All of this says to her children:

In that time of your life when you are with me, I decide what happens. If your father has a problem with what, he and I will settle it. But anything that comes through you does not count. It does nothing. Affects nothing. You can say it or not, whatever you want, it makes no difference.

WHO'S TELLING THE TRUTH?

"Mom says that it was your fault that the twins and I had to wait a half hour at the skating rink. She says she told you that you were supposed to be there at six-thirty. She says she told you that we would end a half hour early today."

Let's say that their mother really had not mentioned it, only thought she had, or simply was shifting the blame for the children's extra wait.

Again a normal response might be:

More Joys of Being in the Middle

"No, your mother did not tell me. I'm sorry you had to wait."

This is a simple statement of fact and not actually wrong. But it still puts the kids in the middle because it asks them to judge which parent is telling the truth.

I don't know who to believe. Mom or Dad.

So maybe Cherie goes back to her mother.

"Dad says you didn't tell him."
"Well, I did."

Maybe Cherie doesn't bring it up at all. Either way she is in the middle, with each parent asking her to believe one side of the story. So how can her father keep her out of it?

"Mom says that it was your fault that the twins and I had to wait a half hour at the skating rink. She says that she told you that we would end a half hour early today and you were supposed to be there at six-thirty."
"I'm sorry you had to wait. Your mother and I obviously had a mix-up about the time."

This answer neither defends nor blames. There is no question of fault at all. It simply says there was a problem and ends it with that. The response says that there was a problem between the parents and recognizes that the problem is their responsibility and has nothing to do with the kids. The "whom do I believe?" question is completely removed.

But what if the kids try to keep this issue alive?

"Well, we had to wait a half hour and Mom says it was your fault."

Again, do not get into it.

"I'm sorry you had to wait. Your mom and I had a misunderstanding about the time."

It takes them out of the argument—refuses to get into it.

Or Jason to his mother:

"Dad says that the reason you don't talk to Aunt Marianne anymore is because you owe her and Uncle Tom five hundred dollars. Dad says you're never going to pay them back."

"No, I did pay Marianne. Our not seeing each other is for different reasons."

Again, this seems okay, but the problem is that it says their father is a liar.

Well, he is, and they should know it.

Unfortunately, that kind of response puts your child right back into the middle of things: "Who tells the truth—Mom or Dad?"

Better:

"I don't see your aunt because we don't get along anymore."

This response neither denies nor admits the accusation about the five hundred dollars. It simply says that the subject is something that Jason's mother will not discuss.

"It was because of the five hundred dollars, wasn't it?"
"It's not something you need to know about."

Even if they persist.

"You should pay her the five hundred dollars." (Which Jason's mother has not said she owed.)
"It is not something I will discuss."

But if Jason's mother doesn't defend herself, won't Jason think that she cheated his aunt out of the five hundred dollars?

Dad's right. Mom was dishonest.

But that's not the message the vast majority of children take from a parent's refusal to answer an accusation. They don't care enough to think that way. In this case, the five-hundred-dollar loan is Jason's father's issue, not Jason's.

What do I care about whether Mom owes Aunt Marianne five hundred dollars? What does that have to do with me?

And again, if Jason's mother simply refuses to get into it any further, it dismisses Jason from the case. He is allowed to drop the whole thing and move on.

Gosh, this topic doesn't seem to be going anywhere. No matter what I say, Mom won't get into it. I guess I'll go on to something else.

"Mom, why can't we go to Burger Barn?"

The alternative, an approach in which Jason's mother says that his father's story is not true, unfortunately only leads to trouble. A denial picks up on the very combative issue raised by Jason's father. Whether the five hundred dollars was paid pack or not is now officially put on the table as an ongoing topic of disagreement between Jason's parents, with him in the middle. It really is better to keep him out of it.

An unfortunate aftermath of divorce is that emotional attachment to one's ex doesn't die the day the divorce is final. It often transforms itself into bad feelings between both parents. Feelings that constantly fuel the ongoing war between you and your ex.

"Dad says all you ever think is of yourself. He says it's what wrecked your marriage."

"Why did you have to get a divorce?"

"Dad, Mom says that the only reason you won't switch about Thursday nights is that you want to make things difficult for her on purpose."

Their words cry for an answer. But don't touch it.

"I'm sorry your mother feels that way."
"She says you do it on purpose because you still hate her for divorcing you."
"I'm sorry your mother feels that way."

And no more. Take the kids out of the middle. End it.

Children as Reporters and Secret-Keepers

"So how was it over at your dad's?"
  "Good. We had a good time."
"What did you do?"
  "Nothing too much. You know. Usual stuff."
"Was Karen there?"
  "Yeah, most of the time. She came over Saturday morning."
"Were Justine and Lisa with her?"
  "Yeah, I like them. Justine's funny."
"Did Karen and your father say anything about her moving in?"
  "No."
"But she and the girls did stay over Saturday night?"
  "Yeah."
"Does that make you uncomfortable—Karen and your father sleeping together in the same room? They do, don't they?"
  "Yeah."
"Does it make you uncomfortable?"
  "I don't know."

"Carla, when you go over to your mom's, I'd appreciate it if you didn't mention that we got the new big-screen TV. There's nothing wrong with my getting it. But you know how your mother always makes a big fuss every time I spend money on anything except support payments to her. And I know you don't like it when your mother and I are fighting with each other. So it really would make things easier for everybody if you just didn't mention the TV. Okay?"

Parents often want to use their children as sources of information about their ex. They also want their children *not* to pass certain information in the *other* direction.

But it's a problem. I worry about what goes on when the kids are at their father's. And how am I going to know what's going on unless I ask? Their father certainly isn't going to tell me anything.

There is nothing wrong with asking kids what they did when they were with their other parent if you ask in the same way that you would ask what they did when they spent a night at a friend's house.

"How was it at your dad's?"
"Good. We made spaghetti. I made the meatballs. They came out good."

Problems arise only when the information sought is not really about them or their visit, but about the other parent.

I wish Mom didn't ask me things about Karen. I know Mom doesn't like her. But when Mom always asks me like she does, I feel I'm telling on Dad. And I don't want to do anything that would get him mad at me. But if I don't tell Mom everything she asks about, I know she'll get upset.

As discussed repeatedly in this book, parents have very little actual control over the other parent or over what goes on during the time when the kids are with that parent. Usually, the more you ask in the role of detective and the more information you get, the more you tend to carry on about it. Rarely is there anything constructive you can do anyway. So all things considered, not knowing is probably best for everybody.

But what if there really is something damaging to the kids going on?

A simple statement to one's kids can be good insurance:

"If there is anything that worries you or scares you at your dad's, you need to always tell me."

Not that they always will, but usually they do.

And what about the secrets? You can't do much to protect your kids against having to be secret-keepers if your ex puts them in that role and makes them uncomfortable doing so. However, you can help them from your end by saying something like this:

"It's okay if you tell Mom what goes on here. I don't mind. Don't worry. There aren't any secrets here. And if there are things that you're not comfortable telling me from your Mom's, that's okay too. If there is something that scares you or really worries you, please tell me. But otherwise, there is nothing you need to tell me unless you want to."

A simple statement like this—if you really mean it—frees kids from most of their burden as reporters, informers, and secret-keepers. In turn, this frees them from feeling like part of a drama between their two parents, and that's always a relief.

Anthony E. Wolf

When Your Ex and You No Longer Speak

I know I shouldn't use the kids as messengers, but whenever their father and I talk, we end up in a shouting match. We simply cannot talk about even the simplest things. I don't like going through the kids, but I don't see where we have a choice.

Sometimes putting your kids in the middle is simply a practical matter. If communication between parents has absolutely broken down, if they cannot talk without arguing, they often use their kids as messengers for making arrangements.

"Dad, Mom's on the phone. She says her car broke down and she has to borrow Aunt Trish's and she won't be here for an hour."

Flexibility is a luxury for those who can communicate. If negotiation is beyond the patience of a particular set of parents, the less need for getting the kids involved, the better. Usually what works best for these parents is that all arrangements are very clearly spelled out and written down. Using the kids to make arrangements in and of itself probably does little damage. At least it's not putting them directly in the middle of a feud. Obviously, it is best if parents can talk to each other, but if that's not possible, using the kids for making arrangements can be a necessary alternative.

Child Support

Child support is one of the most emotionally charged issues between divorced parents—and for good reason. It is also an issue that has a direct effect on children and, more often than not, an issue that readily puts kids in the middle.

"Mom, can I have my birthday party at Fun Burger like Tracy did?"
"No, I'm sorry, Janelle, it just costs more than we can afford."

More Joys of Being in the Middle

"But we could afford it if Dad gave us more child support, couldn't we?"

"I don't know. We might."

"But it's not fair that he doesn't give us enough child support. It's not fair that I can't get the same stuff as my friends."

If you feel your ex-spouse is not being fair about child support and that your children are suffering in some way because of the unfairness, you can be easily tempted to say things like

"I know your father loves you, but I do think he could afford to give us more money. It would not hurt him. Yes, I do think it would make a difference for a lot of things that we can't afford now."

Or worse, which certainly most people would *like* to say:

"You're right. He's been cheating us all along, especially you. Your dad is the most selfish man in the world. He doesn't deserve a child like you. I get sick every time I think about the mistake I made in marrying him. And you know what? Tell him that. He deserves to hear it directly from you."

However, no matter how maddening the situation, to bring one's children into the child support issue only pulls them down and doesn't help get the ex to pay up.

But I do feel their father has cheated me and he's cheated the kids. I don't see why they shouldn't know it. They do lose out because their father would rather spend the money on himself than on his children—money he can afford. I don't see why he should not be made responsible in their eyes for something he has done to them.

If kids get in the middle of a child support conflict, the only thing that they get out of it is pain. As in the middle of other conflicts between their divorced parents, they are pulled out of the safe world of childhood and into a disturbing world of adult worries, conflicts, and feelings—a world that no child can handle. They are also forced to pit one parent against the other and take sides.

"Dad, you're not fair to us. You get to have all kinds of stuff, and me and Mom and Kendall don't get half of what we should."

Or maybe in her head:

"Why did you have to get a divorce?"

Dad really isn't fair. If he loved us right, he wouldn't be so selfish.

And when kids take sides, one parent must lose. But, of course, it is not really the parent who loses.

"I hate Daddy for not giving us enough child support."

The child is now the loser, because there is no longer Daddy to love and be loved by.

Much better to say, though hard, would be this:

"Child support issues are between your father and me. I know you're disappointed that you can't have a party like Tracy's."
"I am and it's Daddy's fault. Even if you don't say so, I know that you think it."
"That's between your father and me."

If you don't get into it, the disappointment about the party will fade, as will the child support issue. Maybe it will reappear the next time Janelle gets disappointed about not being able to have something because you can't afford it. However, the issue doesn't stay in her head as a real ongoing concern or get transformed into an ongoing taking-sides issue between Daddy and Mommy. The money issues are relegated to the much more minor category of fusses one makes when not getting one's way—child issues.

If and when child support issues again arise, if Janelle's mother keeps her daughter out of it, repeatedly stating that the problem is between her father and her mother, Janelle will gradually learn.

There's no point in talking to Mom about Dad not giving us enough money, because she always says the same thing. She won't even talk about it.

Rather than Janelle's getting mad and frustrated by her mother's never getting into it, she is also free not to get into it. One day Janelle might look back and think that her father was a bastard for his selfishness about child support, but maybe not. The issues of child support—a source of great pain for her mother—will for her be only vague memories with little feeling connected to them, not a major theme of her childhood at all.

I'll tell you one thing. I'm not going to just let their father continue getting away with what he's doing. He's constantly missing payments. He has enough money. But he thinks he can get away with not paying, seeing the kids—who adore him, in their eyes he can do no wrong—and nothing's going to happen to him.

If another parent is not meeting a financial obligation to you and your child, then you should do what you can to get what is your and your child's due.

But then I'm the bad guy. And don't think their father won't say that to them. I just can hear them: "Please, Mommy, don't send Daddy to jail."

But again, that is between you and your ex.

"I am doing what I think is best. It is between your father and me."

"No, it's not. Not if Daddy's in jail."

"What happens with child support is between your father and me."

If you stay firm and keep them out of the child support wars, though those wars may rage all around them, they are spared.

SETTING THE RECORD STRAIGHT

Remember that gut-wrenching need to set the record straight mentioned briefly earlier? In many of the situations we've looked at in this chapter, that urge was alive and well. But here's a closer look in both major and minor situations where setting the record straight seems impossible to resist.

Becky needs to understand that it was not my fault that she missed out on going to her friend Danielle's birthday party, that it was her mother who wouldn't switch her times around, that it was not me who was the inflexible one. I don't want Becky blaming me for something that was her mother's fault, not mine.

Or remember Aunt Marianne's five hundred dollars:

I can't believe him. I don't talk to Marianne because she's been openly hostile to me since the divorce. The five hundred dollars was money he borrowed from them way before we got separated to help pay for repairs to my car that we needed at the time. And we did pay the five hundred dollars back out of the tax refund. I can't believe he's bringing that up to the kids.

But sometimes the issues aren't minor. Sometimes they're as major as they can be, such as accusations about the breakup of the marriage that need to be set straight.

"Mom says you were the reason for the divorce. You weren't nice to her and you cheated on her with other women."
I cheated on her?! I wish I had. All she did was rant and rave at me about anything and everything. And she was insanely jealous. I don't know why I stayed around as long as I did.

A failed marriage can leave you with a deep feeling that your ex did you wrong. Now your ex goes on, has a nice life, and the kids still unconditionally love him or her. They have no sense that your ex was ever at fault. How can you not feel that it's just not fair? How can you not feel that your ex is getting away with having his or her cake and eating it too?

"Mom, Dad says that the reason he didn't give us ice skates for Christmas, like he said he would, was that he couldn't afford it because you went to court and raised his child support payments. Besides that, he says you spent the extra money on the new furniture for your living room and not on us."

It totally sickens me. There he is, living with Lana, having a good time, with all his money, which I should be getting more of—but he lied in court—and now he comes off to the kids like he's Mr. Perfect and I'm the problem person. He's getting away with everything and they don't see it.

If your ex is not playing fair, it's very hard not to want the kids to see how matters really stand. As I said earlier, you don't want them to judge you badly. And it's not that you actually want your kids to think badly of your ex. Well, maybe you do sometimes. But what you really want is that truly in their hearts they understand that you do care about them, do try to do what's best for them, and do try to do what you think is right.

However, the absolute truth is that kids like it better, as discussed throughout this chapter, if you do not put them in the middle—even regarding the undeniably true reasons for the divorce. It may be hard to understand, but explanations designed to set them straight do not raise your standing with them one bit. All those explanations ever accomplish is to pull them down *once again* into that emotionally draining mess that darkens their life and that they absolutely hate.

All I want is that Dad likes me and is nice to me. I don't care about any of this other stuff.

Regarding the mother's accusations about the father's cheating, whether they are true or not, her child derives no benefit from getting pulled into that discussion. It's best just to say:

"I know your mom feels bad about the divorce. But what went on is between your mother and me."

"You did cheat on her, didn't you?"

"What went on is between us."

"You did. You did cheat on her."

"What went on is between your mom and me."

The Devil and Elaine

Often it can seem that the only thing that really would remedy the deep sense of unfairness would be if something really bad happened to your ex—not an uncommon fantasy—like going to jail, or ending up a pathetic penniless bum, or developing a dreadful disease. And were that to happen, it would be experienced as a relief and a fitting resolution to all the unfairness. Terrible to say, but true.

Suddenly out of nowhere Elaine found herself confronted by a gentleman wearing a bright red suit who had two small horns coming out of his forehead.

"Hello, Elaine."

"Are you the devil?"

"It's one name I'm called."

"What are you doing here?"

"I have been so concerned about the unfairness of your divorce situation that free of charge I will grant you a special wish."

"Are you sure I'm not going to have to pay for it? Like you get some kind of tiny piece of my soul?"

"Totally free, Elaine. Trust me. My reward is in the wish. If you want, but only if you tell me to, Harry — Mr. Living-the-good-life, and you're stuck with all the bad stuff—will suddenly develop chronic arthritis so that he has very bad pain whenever he walks or tries to lift anything. Pain so bad that it robs his life of joy. Just say the word, Elaine. After all, it's only fair."

"That sounds a little harsh. Can we do it just Tuesdays and Fridays?"

"Certainly, whatever you say."

"And nobody will know that it was because I wished it?"

"Not a soul."

It would be hard to resist.

As I said before, short of making a deal with the devil, the sense of unfairness can be very tough to deal with. There are times when the unfairness can scream out at you and you feel that you *must* set it straight with your kids. But they will only lose if you do.

THE TIME OF RECKONING

Parents who, for the most part, keep their kids out of the battles, who take the high road, as hard as that might be, do, almost always, come to benefit in the end. As one's children get older—especially once they reach adolescence and young adulthood—they view the question of which parent was right or wrong from a totally new perspective. In their hearts, most never cared about which parent was right or wrong. A change comes even with those who perhaps did side with one parent. Now the whole matter shifts from whose argument about blame was the more persuasive to which parent handled the divorce in the more parentlike manner—that is, in the manner best for the kids. Which parent tried to keep them out of it? The whole ball game has changed.

I used to resent Dad for leaving us. I always felt Mom and I were victims of his selfishness. But the truth is that after the divorce, he always treated me well and he never got into the stuff about what

Setting Them Straight about Your Ex

went on between him and Mom, which Mom did constantly. I mean, I still love Mom and all. But I can see that she was the one who was more immature about dealing with the divorce, that she was the selfish one, because she used me to try to make her feel better about her feelings about the divorce.

They are very thankful to you for not bringing them into it.

8

Day to Day with Both Parents

VISITATION—WHAT'S BEST?

What kind of visitation plan is best for kids? If equally divided time with each parent is possible, is that the best? Or is true half-and-half not a good idea? Is every weekend better than every other weekend? Some days during the week? Weekends and one night a week? One month here, one month there?

There is no magic formula, but there doesn't have to be.

"What do you want, Jimmy?"

"I want to see both my mom and my dad as much as I can. When I'm at Dad's, I miss Mom, and when I'm at Mom's, I miss Dad. Sort of. I don't miss them all of the time. But sometimes."

What kids want most is, of course, both parents—although at any given moment when they are with either parent, and regardless of specific visitation arrangements, most kids really are content. The one exception is when there is one parent whom they rarely get to see. Children in these situations often express a wish to be able to see more of that parent. So in most cases, questions regarding the specific amount of time children should spend with each parent are not quite getting to the heart of the matter.

What matters most, if two parents want to be a true part of their child's life, is that their child does get to have a significant amount of time with each parent. Exactly how much time doesn't matter much. The child doesn't have a stopwatch and doesn't want one. I'm talking about when both parents have been in a significant parenting role *all along*. When that has not been the case, when the division has been unequal, it would not be good for the child to find himself or herself spending most of the time in the home of the parent who up to then had been in the distinctly lesser role. That would be unsettling. If there truly has been one main parenting figure, then it is in the child's best interest—all things being equal—that that parent remain as the main parenting figure after the separation.

In short, the division of visitation time should be in line with the respective parenting roles before the separation.

But what is the best arrangement for Veronica?

Who knows. If a child gets a lot of both parents, trying to figure out what would be exactly best is probably impossible.

But I only want to do what's best for her.

But most of the time that's not completely true. What most parents want in regard to visitation schedules is what they want. Most visitation schedules for a given child, more often than not, are about bargaining and negotiating between parents—what they want, what works for them, what they are comfortable with, and what each parent can live with. Which is fine.

In fact, if there is a conflict over visitation, children should consider themselves lucky because they are usually the guaranteed winners. Most visitation arguments between parents are about getting *more*, not less, of their child's time.

When parents simply cannot agree about a visitation schedule, it can be helpful to bring in a professional who may have thoughts about why a particular arrangement is best for a given child or children.

Dr. Finwriter has spelled out in his very detailed report what he feels is best in the way of visitation for Jackie, Tracy, and Terri. He has set down a very specific schedule and very detailed reasons why this schedule is best.

If nothing else, such an intervention—even where both partners may not agree with the recommendations—can supply a resolution that was beyond what the parents could do on their own.

I don't agree with his recommendations, but if he says that this is best for the kids, what can I do? His report is fifty-seven pages long.

Kids want and need easy access to both parents. They want and need significant time with both parents. So if your kids' visitation schedule provides those two things, it will work for them. The rest depends on what will work for you.

UNDERMINING YOUR RULES

"Who's that?"

"Lana. I met her at the bus station."

"What's that you're carrying?"

"That's my bag of drugs."

"Are you crazy? Get her and that out of this house this instant!"

"But, Mom, Dad always lets me bring strange women and drugs up to my room when I'm at his house."

Maybe not women and drugs, but—no question—the rules often do differ.

"But, Dad, I can't fall asleep this early on a Saturday. When I'm at Mom's, we always get to stay up to till eleven.

It's like all the rules that I have are out the window when they are at their mother's. There it's just fun and games. They eat snacks that I don't allow, they watch TV programs they know they're not supposed to, and they stay up as late as they want. And then I get the fallout. They fuss at me about my rules because their mother lets them do whatever they want. She's completely undermining all the limits that I set with the kids.

This is a big problem for many divorced parents: One set of rules with one parent, a completely different set of rules with the other parent, and the children always fussing at the parent with the stricter rules.

"But, Dad, it's not fair. Mom says we never have to."

It drives me crazy. How am I supposed to get them to have any control at all when their mother undermines everything I do? How am I supposed have any control when there's no consistency of rules between us?

The rule about consistency is that there does *not* have to be consistency. It is *not* necessary.

But how are the children ever going to learn any rules if the rules keep changing from place to place? How can I have rules that are going to work if none of them exist when they are with their mother?

At quite an early age, children learn about different rules with different people and in different situations. For example, by three years old most kids easily handle the differences in rules for home or preschool or with a sitter. Even when parents are not divorced, they often don't have the same rules. Their kids learn and use those two different sets of rules to their best advantage: what I can get away with with Dad, what I can get away with with Mom.

Mom gets mad if I don't wash my hands before eating. Dad couldn't care less. Dad makes a big fuss about putting my feet on the couch, so I take them down whenever he comes in the room. But Mom doesn't even notice.

That behavior is neither bad nor good, but simply what human children do. They always push for a better deal if they think they can get it, and in that pursuit they will use the best weapons possible. All children will try or say anything if it works in getting them out of doing what they do not feel like doing. By experience, they learn which responses prove to be winners and which do not. If they find a winner, they stay with it. Fortunately, parents have a very effective weapon to combat these tactics.

"But at Dad's I don't have to brush my teeth *every* night."
"How nice for you that you don't have to do it at your father's. But here you do."

It doesn't matter at all what the rules are with their other parent. What matters is what your rules are and that they cannot undermine your rules by clever fussing.

"But it's not fair. Dad doesn't make us do it. Why should we have to do it here?"
"I want you to brush your teeth now."
"But it's not fair. At Dad's . . ."
"You heard me, Jessica."

They eventually learn that the "I don't have to do it at Dad's" argument is ineffective. However, this doesn't guarantee they'll stop their fussing and carrying on, or that they won't try a new tactic:

"Why did you have to get a divorce?"

Shucks, I guess that line isn't working. I'll have to think of something else.

"Mom, I really don't feel so good. Can I lie down?"

If "But at Dad's . . ." always gets "That's nice, but *here* this is the rule," and if you don't pick up on further fussing, then "But at Dad's" fades away as a favorite manipulation because it has not proved effective. You have not allowed it to be. And maybe they do what you want them to do, or maybe they don't.

"But, Mom, I still don't think I can brush my teeth. I think there's something wrong with my hand. It can't pick up stuff right. Look at it. It's all funny. I can't hold a toothbrush. I can't. Look, I keep dropping it."

But at least their resistance to *your* rules has nothing to do with what goes on with the other parent, and everything to do with you—which, although not always so easy, is how it should be.

I Don't Always Want to Be the Bad Guy

"Daddy's nicer than you. You always yell at us."

I really worry that they don't like me as much as they do their father. I worry that they may grow up actually thinking that I was the mean parent and their father the nice one. What am I supposed to do, let them do whatever they want?

This is a tough one. Often, one parent—especially the one who has the kids the majority of the time—ends up being the one who does most of the day-to-day "pick up your room," "don't punch your sister" parenting. The other parent doesn't have to do as much of that because the time he or she spends with the kids is more limited and usually more recreational—that is, on weekends. They simply need to do far less.

Do the kids actually like the parent with the fewer rules better? We can ask.

"Do you really like your dad better?"

"I don't know."

"But you just said you did. You said he was nicer than your mom."

"Yeah, well, my mom always is bossing me about stuff and I get mad."

"So you do like your dad better?"

"I don't know. I like his rules better. And I wish Mom wouldn't yell at me about every little thing so much."

"So what are your true feelings? Who do you like better?"

"I don't know. I mean, I guess I love them both the same. But I do get mad at Mom. She should have rules more like Dad's."

In the long run, they definitely won't love you less for having been the parent who fussed at them more. Looking back, they will see it as you see it now.

"No, I know that you had to be the one to nag us because you were the one who mainly was in charge. You were only doing your job. You were a good mom."

Or:

"I mean, I loved Dad. But you were my mom. He wasn't the person I lived with."

Actually, they see it that way even at the time that it's all happening. They would even say so if they didn't feel that by admitting it they might thereby lose even the tiniest piece of leverage.

But what do you get *now* as recompense for the fact that you are most often in the enforcer role? Perhaps simply the knowledge that you're being the responsible one, that it's you, not the other parent, who is more important in the raising of your children. Maybe truly knowing that can make up for what sometimes feels so unfair.

Not really.

What about knowing that your kids love you, will always love you, even though what you often get from them day-to-day can be downright nasty? Maybe that can make the unfairness feel better?

No, not that either. So what can make the unfairness of it feel okay?

Often the way it works out *is* unfair because the sometimes-bad-guy role simply comes with being the main custodial parent. You're stuck with being the bad guy while he's Mr. Nice Guy. You get to see the nasty side of your kids while he gets model behavior from them. But underneath their bad behavior, they do love you as much as, if not more than, their other parent. And that's the truth.

CARRYOVER PUNISHMENT

"Dad, Mom said I'm supposed to give you this note."

Dear Tom, Please make sure B.J. sees no TV tonight. I told him clearly about the consequences if he didn't pick up his room before going with you this weekend. He didn't. He was told a number of times.
Thanks,
Marge

She's always doing this. When I get the kids she sticks me with some kind of punishment or something else that interferes with my being able to have a nice time with them.

But what else can I do? I want B.J. to clean up his room. If his father doesn't carry out the punishment, B.J. knows that he can delay cleaning up his room until it's time to go and nothing will happen to him. He can simply get away with not cleaning up his room.

In most situations, carryover punishments are not good because they burden the other parent with enforcing a rule or decision he or she was not a part of and is not necessarily in support of. They can easily create friction between the parents, with the kids definitely caught in the middle. They also disregard the general rule that the responsibility for control when your kids are with you is *yours*—and vice versa.

Although most of the time carryover punishments are not a good idea, they can work if both parents are in total agreement that the crimes with one parent can be paid for when the kids are with the other. For this to work, both parents need to feel that it's a good idea. Both must *want* to do it. Otherwise, carryover punishments are a mistake.

Without the clear agreement with the other parent, if B.J.'s mother wants to hand out a no-TV punishment for not cleaning up his room, that punishment needs to happen during *her* time with B.J.—when he is back with her. The punishment can wait.

If it's a long period before B.J. is to return, if he'll be away for three weeks with his father on vacation, forget the punishment. It's not fair to the children or their father that their time together should begin with a punishment. It's also not useful to B.J.'s mother to have to carry over a punishment from so long ago when she gets the kids back. In this case, B.J. gets away with not cleaning up his room, which is not the end of the world.

DISNEY DAD

"Mom, Mom, it was so cool. Dad let me steer his jet and then we went to this great restaurant where they have all-you-can-eat ostrich burgers. What's for supper?"

Many Parents Find It Hard to Let Go

"Flour-and-water pudding."

"Again?"

"No, this time I have a special treat for you and Lena. Because I've taken the third job working in the sewers both of you are going to get three raisins mixed into your pudding."

Perhaps it is not quite as bad as the above, but there can be a big difference in the nature of the time spent with two parents.

Anthony E. Wolf

When he sees the kids they always do something fun. They go to the movies. They go out to eat. They go to Video World at the mall. And he gets them stuff all the time. I'd love to buy them things just for the hell of it, but I don't have the money. I barely have enough for essentials, and sometimes that's close.

One huge frustration for many separated or divorced parents is that one of them gets the "fun and games" role. If one parent does most of the real day-to-day child raising, the other—often the father, who may in fact also have more disposable money—gets the purely recreational role of Disney Dad. But even though your role seems harder and Disney Dad's more fun, don't make the mistake of thinking that the Disney Dad role breeds more caring or more love in one's children.

There is a powerful truth about what children want and need from their parents. Though they may hound you for presents, games, toys, dolls, clothes, or trips to exciting places, these are not the stuff of nurturing. In fact, too much focus on wanting and getting can actually end up depriving kids of the nurturing that they really need. If all one does is go after stuff and excitement, that quest can come to block out all else. It can even create an inner emptiness.

Genuine nurturing comes from *being with*—from talking to them, listening to them, touching them, and caring for them. And, yes, it even comes from repeated requests to pick up their clothes and take out the garbage. Nurturing comes from the back-and-forth of human caring. That and that alone is nurturing.

Which has more of a feel for actual human closeness, for personal contact—a child playing a video game at a mall whose parent is patiently waiting outside the arcade area for the child to finish or a parent and child sitting next to each other watching TV, doing errands with the kid riding along in the car, walking down the street for a pizza, eating meals together, helping with homework?

In fact, kids feel more love for, are happier with, and get more out of a relationship that might seem rather mundane compared to Disney Dad's constant circus. Where the relationship with one parent is all about getting and spending and doing, kids feel far less secure about their *personal* relationship with that parent.

So don't try to measure up to Disney Dad. You do not need to. Besides, kids will always ask for stuff.

"Can we go play miniature golf? Dad always takes us to play miniature golf."

Maybe you will take them to play miniature golf or maybe you won't. It *is* nice to go out sometimes and do fun things together. But if you choose not to, don't worry about it. They love to play miniature golf, but this has nothing to do with their love for you.

Still, the contrast between you and Disney Dad can at times be pretty hard to take.

"Mom, Ivan keeps trying to pull the hairs off my six-foot Teddy that Daddy just bought for me. Mom, make him stop."

I WANT TO LIVE AT DAD'S

"Christopher, leave your sister alone."

"I'm not doing anything."

"Christopher, I said to stop it."

"But Erika wrecked my building."

"Christopher, I do not want to have to keep telling you. Leave your sister alone."

"But she doesn't leave me alone."

"Yes I do, you started it."

"You stay out of this, Erika. I will handle it."

"But Christopher is a liar."

"Christopher, I want you to go to your room."

"But I didn't do anything."

"Yes you did, Christopher, you liar."

"I'm going to kill her, Mom."

Anthony E. Wolf

"Christopher, go to your room."

"Why is it always me? Why do you always say I do everything? It's always me. You always pick on me. I hate it here. I do. I want to live at Dad's. I really do. I want to live at Dad's."

I do everything I can. I try to be as good a parent as I can be. But it's not easy, especially since I've been on my own. Sometimes I lose my temper with them. But I really do my best. Apparently that's not good enough. When Christopher says he wants to live at his father's, it's like I've failed.

When children spend most of the time living in the home of one parent, somewhere along the line they'll usually express the wish to live with their other parent. When they say it, they mean it. At least at that moment.

"Christopher, do you really want to live at your dad's?"
"Yes, I hate it here."

A lie detector will show he's telling the truth.

"Why don't you want to live at your mother's?"
"Because Mom is mean and Erika is a lying brat."

But were we to ask him the same question at another time, when he has not just been yelled at by his mother and told to go to his room, we would almost invariably get a different answer.

"Do you want to go live at your dad's?"
"I don't know."
"What do you mean, you don't know? I thought you said you wanted to live at your dad's."
"I don't know."

Now a note of concern is coming into Christopher's voice. *Is he talking about me moving to Dad's house for real?*

"So where to you want to live?"
"I think I want to stay here."
"So why did you say that you wanted to live at your dad's?"
"Because I was mad at Mom and Erika was a brat."
"So you don't really want to live at your dad's?"
"No."

Again, a lie detector would show he's telling the truth, because far and away the most common reason children will say they want to live with the other parent is that, at that moment, they're not getting their way.

So if your child says that he or she wants to live with the other parent, stop and look at the situation. If this announcement comes at a time when they don't like what's going on, think long and hard before you take them too seriously.

"Christopher, go to your room."
"I hate it here. I hate you. I hate Erika. I want to live at Dad's."
"Christopher, go to your room."
"I want to live at Dad's. I do."

But what if he really means it? What if he says it and it really seems to be something that he wants?

Later I will talk about when children actually do switch homes —mainly a phenomenon of the teenage years. But unless you seriously want to make the switch *and* that switch is wanted by your child's other parent, what your children say or even want at any given time is a nonissue. The choice of which parent a child lives with should be the parents' decision—assuming that this is not a custody battle in the courts, which is a whole other matter.

Children need to know that they live in a home with a parent who will stay with them, regardless of what their feelings about where they want to live may be at any given moment. It is not in a child's best interest to have the power to decide. Children need to know that where they live day-to-day is out of their hands. Therefore, even when you might think they really would like to switch, unless you decide that this is what you want, where they live must be your decision, not their preference.

"Mom, I do want to live at Dad's."
"No, you are still going to live here."
"But I want to live at Dad's. He says it would be okay."
"No, you are going to live here."

This has become a closed issue, and as with other closed issues, they accept it and go back to living their lives.

LITTLE MEN

Some children can be especially difficult.

Whatever I say to David he always answers back. He argues about everything. He has this attitude as if I don't have the right to tell him to do anything. He constantly puts me down, often calling me stupid. He is forever saying how he likes his father better than me and how he wants to live with him.

Often when boys live with their mother after a divorce—especially boys who were fairly willful to begin with—they begin to see themselves very much as the man of the house. A part of their personality which was always present comes to dominate.

I'm not a boy. I'm a man.

Now that their father is out of the home, they prefer to see themselves as full-status, manly adults, even though they are not. They strongly resent a mother who treats them like the child they are.

"Why did you have to get a divorce?"

"You can't tell me to pick up my room."

More simply, they vigorously resent being bossed around. They feel it's a put-down, a challenge to their self-appointed role as a man and an adult equal in the house.

"You don't have the right to give me orders."

Maddeningly, the boys are much more respectful with their father. They identify with their father as "we men" and do not mind obeying, viewing their father as possessing a strength and authority that may or may not have anything to do with their father's actual personality.

So maybe he would be better off living at his father's?

Occasionally such changes can work out for the best. But more often than not, if he does actually switch households, the magic eventually wears off. He will start challenging his father's authority because he now feels it is his father who is putting him down by giving him orders.

Living with a rude and disrespectful child can be tough, but what works best—no question—is an understanding that you are the parent and he is the kid and, though a part of him absolutely hates that role, it's not changing. And where parents do hang in there, do stay in the parent role, are firm, do not try too much to explain or justify, and above all do not battle with the child with the challenging attitude—it usually works out. You are the parent and a part of him, a healthier, more productive part, still wants to be a child with a strong parent. He may strongly challenge your right to be the boss, but it is a battle he wants to lose. He wants a strong parent. It's just that he'll make you prove it.

"Kyle, please play with the hard rubber ball outside only."
"Why? It's not hurting anything."

"Kyle, we've been through this before. Do not play with that hard rubber ball in the house."

"But I'm not hurting anything. Besides, it's my house just as much as yours. You can't tell me to do anything."

"Kyle, please put the ball away."

And if a parent stays firm, doesn't blow up, and above all doesn't get caught up in all of the provocative challenges the child may throw at the parent, the child usually will comply.

"Thank you, Kyle."
"It wasn't hurting anything."

Although he doesn't admit it, Kyle feels relieved that there is a strong parent in the house.

Oh, I guess I'm not the man of the house. I'm just a boy. Good. In that case I think I'll go play with my action figures.

But there is no question that such kids can be tough to handle. Once their father is out of the home, the part of them that says they are supposed to have full adult status does not succumb easily.

Rules for Holidays, Birthdays, etc.

Ralph, the children's father:

The plan is that Linda is going to pick up Kristen and Emory at five on Christmas Eve and they'll go with her over to their grandmother's—Linda's mother. Then they'll go back to Linda's, where they will spend the night. Christmas morning they will open their presents and get their stockings. Then I will pick them up at ten-thirty so they can come back to my house and get their stockings and open their presents at my house. At two, we'll go over to my sister's for her big Christmas and we'll stay there through Christmas night. The kids love it at my sister's. They really look forward to the chance to spend time with their cousins from Ohio.

Linda:

Ralph was completely unreasonable about Christmas. He knows how special Christmas night has always been at my sister's and how much the kids have always loved it. All I asked for was that I could pick them up at seven-thirty p.m. so they could at least get to see their cousins from Vermont. Ralph knows how much Kristen and Emory idolize the twins. They will have been at his sister's for five and a half hours, which seems like plenty. By seven-thirty their big meal will be long over since they sit down to eat at four. It breaks my heart for them for what they will have to miss out at my sister's.

Holidays. Birthdays. Special occasions. Often, they're trouble. How many family relationships were never quite the same after what happened at the wedding, at the funeral, at Aunt Hilda's house for Thanksgiving, at the Bar Mitzvah? Holidays and special events are wonderful. I am strongly in favor of them. They punctuate life with special times that we look forward to and somehow remember in a special way. But those special occasions also have a way of creating all kinds of hurt feelings, expectations that were not met, and permanent grudges.

Special occasions breed special expectations. Parents are no exception and often have big hopes for holidays and special events —hopes both for themselves and for their kids.

Linda:

Maybe I put too much emphasis on it, but waking up in the morning with Kristen and Emory there and having them go down and get their stockings and open their presents—it's just terribly important to me to be there when they wake up Christmas morning.

You don't know how much that means to me. It was that way when I was a kid, and it's always been that way for Kristen and Emory. But going to my sister's with my kids on Christmas night has always been a part of it too. That's very special for me and I know that it is for the kids.

But if there's another active parent who wishes to be with the kids—and this is good—then you will see less of the kids, including during these special times. It is a loss. It is sad. It is a fact of divorce. Yet the kids, even if they don't get as much time as they'd like everywhere, even if they miss out on a special set of cousins, will still have a good time. The special occasions will still be special. Problems come when parents care too much. Or, worse, when parents suffer too much for them.

You don't know. Emory talks about the twins all year. He really feels bad about not seeing them.

Maybe he does. But Emory looks forward to the holidays and will have a good time even if he misses out on seeing the twins. What swiftly turns special occasions into something altogether different is if injustices, hurt feelings, and special grievances are added into the holiday mix. Emory, who could have gotten used to the idea that he wouldn't see the twins, might not if his mother makes too much out of it. If Emory's mother fusses too much about Emory's disappointment, Emory begins to think that he *should* feel bad about missing the twins.

"Well, gosh, I just about never get to see the twins. I don't see why I can't see them at least a little on Christmas."

Emory then feeds his mother's sense of feeling hurt for him, thereby increasing her anger at his father and ultimately making the whole thing a big mess.

"Why did you have to get a divorce?"

"If his father thinks I'm going to forget this, I most certainly will not. Emory was devastated. His father only thinks of himself. He sure knows how to ruin a Christmas. But I won't make things go easy for him next time."

The best strategy for holidays and special occasions is to have all the arrangements clearly spelled out. In writing if necessary. Flexibility is preferred, but don't count on it. In any case, one or both of you may still not be happy with the final arrangements. There may be no way to split the kids and still do everything that you really care about. It can be disappointing.

But do not get confused. From the kids' standpoint, the arrangements—whatever they are—are not a tragedy. Their special times are still special. What matters to them, what is most special to them, is that they get regular contact with both parents. If on a particular special occasion they do miss out on seeing a particular parent, if they do not get all of the special pieces of each special time, well, it's just not that big a deal for them. Holidays and special occasions get to be problems only when parents make them so.

9

Problems with Visits

RETURNING FROM THE OTHER PARENT'S:
THE SUNDAY NIGHT PHENOMENON

"Mom, Jeremy kicked my galoshes."
"I did not. Kara put them where I could trip on them."
"You're such a baby, Jeremy."
"Mom, Kara called me a baby."

No sooner have brother and sister gotten through the door, returning from a weekend visit at their father's, than a fight breaks out. For the rest of the evening, they're picking at each other, whining, fussing, and being totally uncooperative about everything. They just won't calm down.

What is their problem? Every time they go to visit their father it's the same thing. As soon as they get back they're horrible. And they stay horrible. Sometimes it isn't until they return from school on Monday that things finally get back to normal. Not that the two of them are perfect—they're not—but they're always much worse after visits to their father's.

On top of that, he always says that when they're with him, they're well behaved and rarely fight. I've asked the kids and they say it's true.

Seeing the regularity and predictability with which this phenomenon occurs, the main custodial parent typically draws certain conclusions.

Either

I don't know, I must be doing something wrong. I can't seem to control them as well as he does—which I don't exactly understand, because really I'm tougher than he is.

Or

There must be some kind of problem when the kids are over at their father's. Something is not right when they are there, or there's something about visiting him that's disturbing to the kids. It has to be, because I so clearly see the fallout from the visit every time they come back.

Both of these hypotheses may be true, but there's another reason that, far more often than not, is responsible for the sudden outburst of bad behavior once kids return from visits.

Where one parent has the kids most of the time day-to-day, with the other parent definitely in a lesser role, the two parents typically witness quite different behavior. The parent who gets the kids most of the time gets the babyish, less well-behaved side. This is the parent the kids are most comfortable with and with whom the "baby side" comes out. Conversely, with a parent who spends less time with the children, the same level of intimacy, of comfort, is often not there, and that parent in many cases doesn't see the more babyish, not so well-behaved version of his or her kids. That parent gets to see a much more mature, better-behaved side. It's a natural, perfectly healthy phenomenon.

This phenomenon of good for one parent, definitely not so good for the other often happens even when both parents are still in the home. A child will be uncooperative, whiny, prone to arguing and back talk with his or her mother—or whichever parent is responsible for most of the day-to-day child raising. But for the other parent—the one with whom the child does not feel as comfortable—he or she is much more well-behaved and obedient.

But why do they act up extra badly when they return from being with their father?

Being in the mature mode, which your kids have been in while visiting their other parent, takes energy—just like being at work. Eventually they have to switch to their relaxed, more babyish self to recuperate. They wait until they get home with the parent they are most comfortable with, and then the baby side returns with a vengeance.

Finally, at last, I'm home. Now I don't have to control myself and I'm going to really give it to my baby brat brother.

Any parent who has been through this knows that the unwinding process takes time to fully run its course.

"Mom, I can't sleep. Jeremy's making funny gurgle noises in his room."

"Dad, can't you do anything abut Crystal's eating? It's disgusting. Crystal, you're disgusting."

"I'm too tired to take a bath. I'm too tired."

But there can be a payback of sorts. If children get to live with the one who is not the main custodial parent for an extended period of time—maybe for four weeks in the summer—matters

Returning from Dad's

change. Kids cannot stay in the mature mode indefinitely. It's too much of a strain. On extended visits with the other parent, kids get comfortable enough to allow their baby side to come forth with that parent too.

"I don't understand it, Edith. During the year when the kids were with me they hardly ever fought and they were pretty cooperative. But these four weeks I saw a whole other side of them. I don't know what happened."

What happened was that their father got the baby version of the children that their mother had been getting all along. The fact that they collapse when they get back home after a visit with your ex doesn't mean that either you or your ex is doing something wrong. They are simply relieved to be back home—with you.

GOING BACK AND FORTH

"Mom?"

"What is it, dear?"

"Where's Mr. Snuffles?"

"I don't know, dear. Isn't he in your overnight bag?"

"No, I looked."

"Uh-oh, maybe you forgot to pack him."

"I think I forgot to pack him, Mommy," said Lawrence, a wave of cold terror washing over his body. "I left him at Dad's. YOU HAVE TO GET HIM!"

"But you know your father is away. Even if I went over to his house, I couldn't get in."

"YOU HAVE TO GET HIM!"

"But, dear . . ."

"YOU HAVE TO GET MR. SNUFFLES!"

It is inevitable that shifting back and forth between the homes of two parents is going to entail some rough edges.

"Hello, Grace. You have to drive over here right away with Cynthia's science book."

"I have to do what?"

"You heard me. I have a hysterical child over here. She says she has a science test tomorrow and forgot her book."

"I'm not going to drive a half hour to deliver a science book."

"Grace, you don't understand. I have a hysterical child over here."

Or what is more common (but less dramatic)—missing, wrong, or inadequate clothing:

"Dad, I can't go to school. I don't have any clean underwear."

No question, the constant switching back and forth can be an added inconvenience, an added disruption in a child's life, even at times a source of real problems like the forgotten teddy bear or the needed schoolbook. Even when nothing goes wrong, it cannot be so easy for kids regularly to go back and forth between homes, always having to keep track of what's where and what needs to be brought from one place to the other.

"I have to remember when I go to school today to bring the present for Laurie Ann's party, because Dad's picking me up from school, and even though the party isn't until tomorrow, I won't have a chance to go back to Mom's and get the present."

The best solution that parents seem to come up with is to keep the necessity for item transfers to a minimum. This means having duplicate items of basic clothing and daily-use articles like toothbrushes, hairbrushes, deodorant. Still, there will be hassles. They're the price that kids and parents must pay for the far larger benefit, which is having an ongoing relationship with both parents. If kids are to see a significant amount of both parents after the divorce, it's inevitable there will be an added degree of confusion in their lives.

But kids really do adapt, and the benefits—significant time with both parents—far outweigh the hassles.

"Do you mind all the switching back and forth?"
"I don't know."
"Doesn't it bother you sometimes?"
"I don't know. No. It's okay. Except the time I forgot Mr. Snuffles."

"But even that wasn't so bad, was it? You survived. You got through a night without Mr. Snuffles."

"No, I didn't. I died of a broken heart."

Tough Times at the Other Parent's

"Mom, I like Dad and all, but he's always busy doing stuff when me and Lila go over there. He's never around much. And when he is there, he's always in a bad mood. I'm afraid to say anything because he'll just yell at me. So all I do is sit around and watch TV—there's nothing else to do there anyway. And Sylvia [their stepmother] is always there and she's always telling me, 'Don't do this and don't do that,' and I don't do anything. I don't think she likes kids. All she cares about is the house."

He loves his father, but each time when he's scheduled to go over there, I can see how he gets real quiet. I feel like I'm sending him off to weekend prison camp. When he gets back I always get this long story about how he hated the time there. I keep telling their dad, 'They're your kids,' and how he should spend more of the time paying attention to them. But he never changes anything. Sylvia runs that house. I really wish the kids didn't have to go.

Some children spend time with their other parent that is genuinely unpleasant. There can be lots of reasons for the unpleasantness, some as basic as that they never exactly clicked with that parent or they feel uncomfortable with him or her.

"I don't understand Dad. I never know what to say to him. I always feel he disapproves of me, but I don't know why."

Or the environment can be significantly more harsh than what they're used to.

"Mom's stepkids are so wild they never leave me alone."

"I'm scared being all the way out in the woods where Dad lives. It's so far away from anything. And there's nobody to play with."

"There's no bed for me, so I have to sleep in a sleeping bag on the floor."

Your ex's new partner can create multiple problems. Complaints about mean stepparents are not uncommon and not always fairy tales.

"Mom, when we are over at Dad's, Sylvia doesn't let us do anything. She yells at us for no reason. And yesterday when I said the ketchup tasted funny, she told me to 'shut up.' "
"It's true, she always yells at both me and Clary. And Dad just sits there. He never says anything when Sylvia is mean to us. I hate Sylvia."

Well, it's true. It makes me so upset. Whenever the kids go over to their father's I always hear another Sylvia story. And I know my kids. I know that everything they say is really going on. And Rick, Mr. Passive, he's not going to lift a finger. I should know.
I don't know what to do. It's not fair to the kids to have to deal with her the way she treats them every time they see their father, and he doesn't do a thing.

Sometimes children's complaints about the iniquities that they suffer at the hands of an ex's partner can be less about dislike and suffering over there and more about a nice bonding time with you when they return home. Kids often like to complain about what goes on at the other parent's as part of a comfortable, unwinding, adventure-relating time after coming back home with you. But sometimes the stories are both real and troubling. Maybe an ex's partner couldn't care less about your kids and is often overly harsh with them.

Anthony E. Wolf

"Sylvia won't even let Dad get any kind of special food for us. She says she doesn't want to waste their money on kids who aren't hers. We don't starve. But there's never anything we like to eat. She doesn't like us. Yesterday she said, 'Do you always have to follow me around wherever I go?' and I wasn't doing anything."

You might also hear complaints like this about a stepparent:

"Dad, when we go over to Mom's, it's always Harris who decides everything. He completely bosses Mom around and makes all the rules about us. Since she married him it's been like he's the boss of everything over there. I asked Mom if it was okay if I could make cookies and she said, 'Ask Harris.' It's her house too. And besides, he's not my dad. You are."

This complaint is particularly maddening. They're not his kids. What right has he to boss your kids? What right has she when they're with her to abandon to this other husband her role as their real parent? What can you do about this and other stepparent complaints? If you do not suspect abuse, then the basic "hands off" rule about the other parent's time with your kids applies here as well.

But I can't just sit by and watch the kids go over and suffer at the hands of a person who is not even their parent.

You can talk to your ex. You can write a note if you're not on speaking terms. But, unfortunately, more often than not such communications end up being quite frustrating. Often an ex will simply be turned off and will feel that this is just another example of your interfering:

"There she goes again. Why can't she just get a life?"

Your complaints usually accomplish little and may well get back to your ex's partner, with the almost certain probability of making even more trouble for your kids.

"Those little brats. They just love running back to their mother and painting me as a nagging bitch. Well, if they want a bitch, I'll *show* them a bitch."

Still, if you understand that all of the above may well happen, that your intervention may do little, but regardless feel that you must do something, there are strategies for the best way of presenting your concern.

"The kids have said to me"—and then quote the kids as simply and as accurately as you can: " 'Sylvia's mean to us . . .' "

Then say immediately,

"I'm not there, so I understand that I don't know what really goes on."

You *don't* actually know the whole story, and as much as possible you do not want to attack but to state the kids' reports as best as you know them. As much as possible, you do not want to put your ex on the defensive. The more your ex feels under attack, the less likely it is that he or she will truly hear what you have to say.

"I just thought it was important that you know what the kids are saying."

The one good possibility out of this is that even though your ex may be mad at you for what he or she feels is your interference, he or she may also recognize what may be the truth in your words.

I'll never admit it to Clara, but sometimes Sylvia really is mean to the kids.

And maybe they'll figure out something that they can do to soften their partner's negative impact.

But even under the most unpleasant circumstances at the other parent's, kids usually show a real ambivalence.

"Would you rather not go to your father's?"
"I don't know. I don't want to hurt his feelings. I don't want him to be mad at me. But I really don't like it over there and I hate Sylvia. I do."

They often correctly fear that if they don't go, their other parent would be hurt and mad at them. They worry that as a result they would lose the love of their other parent.

I only have two parents, you know.

Though the time with the other parent may be truly unpleasant, typically it does not do damage and it may have actual benefits. Besides the inherent value of having a second active parent, there's another possible benefit. Time spent with the noncustodial parent can give them a taste of being independent, which includes learning to survive on their own. Unpleasant time spent with the other parent can be a bit like the psychological equivalent of one of those character-building survival courses where they put you on an island with a penknife and a box of matches and you spend a very uncomfortable few days surviving.

"It was great. I only ate roots and I got a big cut on my arm and I got a bad sunburn. I don't think I slept more than two hours because of the mosquitoes. I want to go back next year for the double-torture week where they only give you *one* match."

Do they enjoy the time at Dad and Sylvia's? Maybe not. But they can come away each time with a certain sense of accomplishment and a little more maturity:

"I got through another visit—all on my own. I'm a tough kid."

Maybe they deserve a sweatshirt that says, "I survived another weekend at Dad and mean Sylvia's."

If They Don't Want to Go

"Mom, I don't want to go to Dad's this weekend," said eight-year-old Charlie to his mother.

"Why, Charlie?"

"It's boring there. There's nothing to do. All I do is sit around all day. It's more fun for me if I stay here. I have friends here to do stuff with. There's nobody at Dad's for me to play with at all. I don't want to go."

Well, it is boring there for him. Just like Charlie says. He has no friends there. And he and his dad don't really do a lot together. I don't even think his dad likes the visits any more than Charlie does. I think he just does them because he's afraid of what other people will say if he didn't see Charlie. Mainly, Charlie just sits around and watches TV. I don't blame him for not wanting to go. I wouldn't want to go if I were Charlie. Besides, it can't be really good for him to spend big chunks of time sitting around doing nothing. Why should he have to go if he doesn't want to?

What should parents do if a child doesn't want to go for a scheduled visit to the other parent's—either as dictated by the court or as part of a negotiated visitation agreement between the parents? Should that decision be left up to the child?

First of all, both parents must agree—*really agree*—that it is okay for their children to have a voice in the decision. Then that de-

The Evil Stepmother

cision should be worked out directly between the child and the parent *to be visited.*

"Dad, I don't feel like coming over this weekend."

"You don't?"

"No, I just want to stay at Mom's this weekend. Is that okay? I'll see you next weekend."

"Yeah, I guess so. I'll see you next week."

But Charlie's father might not want to say yes.

"Why did you have to get a divorce?"

I mean, I know it's boring for him when he comes to see me—not as much fun as it is at his mother's. But what am I supposed to do? It's not my fault all his friends are over there. It makes me feel bad when he says he doesn't want to come. It's the one time that I get to be with him, and I don't want to lose it.

In which case Charlie's father can say no.

"Dad, do I have to come this weekend? I just don't feel like it. I just want to stay at Mom's. Can I? Just this weekend?"
"No, Charlie. This is your weekend with me."
"But, Dad, just this time, please?"
"I'll be by to pick you up at the regular time."
"But, Dad . . ."
"I'll pick you up at the regular time."

If Charlie were then to go to his mother:
"Mom, do I *have* to go to Dad's this weekend? Dad says I do, but I really don't feel like it. Just this weekend? Just this once? What's the big deal? Please."

Charlie's mother must not discuss it. Although she might think:

But what if he really doesn't have a good time, doesn't like it at his father's? It's not fair to him to force him to always go there when he hates it, to force him to do something against his will.

Parents need to agree that the child is stuck with whatever arrangements have been made. Charlie's mother must support her ex's decision.

"No, you know this is your weekend with your father."
"But, Mom, I don't want to go this weekend. I really don't want to."
"I'm sorry, Charlie. This is your weekend with your father."

No discussion. No negotiation. When parents are consistently firm and don't go into lengthy discussions, problems centered on visits are significantly reduced.

As we've discussed, if there is not abuse, occasional not-fun times do not cause damage, and they continue an important relationship. However, if children are allowed to decide repeatedly not to see the other parent, in effect rejecting that parent, he or she is likely to drift away.

I know I shouldn't feel that way. But if Danny doesn't care enough about me to want to come over, I can't help it, I start caring about him less too.

Another strong reason that visitation decisions should not be left up to a child is that reluctance or refusal to visit a parent often has nothing to do with not wanting to visit. Not really. Rather, the problem is separating from the main custodial parent.

Kids who are reluctant to separate will give all kinds of reasons for not wanting to go to the other parent's:

"It's so stuffy at Dad's house."

"Baby Brendan cries all the time at night and I can't sleep."

"Gracey [the stepmother] doesn't cook anything I like."

If you can get them to go, they usually have a good time. However, they still might call up and want to come home early.

"Dad said it's okay. Can you pick me up at three instead of six? Please. Please."

When children have separation problems, you need to be firm about getting them to go to the place or engage in the activity from

which they are hanging back, and that includes visits to a noncustodial parent. Children who do not develop enough ability to separate can carry that dependence into adult life. They become too
dependent, unable to separate in those situations and from those
people with whom they should.

But the most important reason that children should not decide
about the visits is that it gives them too much power to elicit strong
feelings inside their parents. And this is not good. Children need
to feel that their behavior—even when at times they are genuinely
nasty—cannot affect their parents' feelings toward them in any significant way. A key piece of a child's basic sense of security is
feeling that, in regard to Mom and Dad, he or she is indeed the
child.

"I mean, I know Mom gets really mad at me for some of the
stuff I do and say. But I know it never really changes how she feels
about me."

When children control visits, they have the power to touch deep
places inside both of their parents. It pulls children up to adult
levels where they do not belong.

The parent who is being rejected thinks:

*Well, Marilyn's finally done it. She's twisted Heather around her
little finger and now the kid doesn't even want to be with me. Well,
screw both of them.*

And the parent with whom the child wants to stay thinks:

*Good, he doesn't want to see his father. He likes me better. Serves
his father right for divorcing me.*

When children have no choice in the matter, they will fight you
less because they learn that their fighting changes nothing. Given
that understanding, parents can then be flexible when they need

to be. For example, exceptions might include your child's being invited to a special birthday party at a friend's where the distance from the other parent's house to the friend's house is too great to be practically convenient, a time when a special aunt is visiting which happens only once a year, or when a child is very sick and moving him to the other parent for the weekend makes little sense. But even when exceptions are made, your child must understand that this is *not* his or her decision, but an exception about which both parents agree. Furthermore, exceptions must be the exception. The general rule must remain: Visiting arrangements are set by the parents and not controlled by a child's choosing and whims.

Teenagers are a necessary exception.

"Dad, do I really have to go to Mom's this weekend? I have lots of homework and I promised Janice I would go over to her house Saturday night."

"But this will be the third time in a row that you've missed."

"Yeah, well, I'm sorry about that. I don't mean to hurt her feelings. I'll go next time."

Well, what am I supposed to do? I just want to hang around with my friends on the weekend. What's wrong with that? That's what normal teenagers do. And when I go over to Mom's, it's too big a hassle to see people, so I just end up sitting around there. It's true, I don't want to hurt her feelings, but what am I supposed to do?

Obviously, both parents can encourage teenagers to go. Both parents can order them to go. Courts can order them to go (which courts rarely actually do). But if a teenager really decides that he or she doesn't want to go on a particular visit to a particular parent, there is little anybody can do to make it happen.

The best plan with teenagers is to keep scheduled visits in place and for both parents to continue to encourage the teenager to go. Contrary to what would be appropriate with younger children and in recognition that adolescents are older and do need to exercise more control over their own lives, it is also good to be flexible and to try to negotiate a plan that the teenager is comfortable with. Regardless, what is definitely a mistake with teens is to try to coerce them to go. All that will do is create resentment toward both parents and accomplish little that is positive.

Teenagers tend to turn away from parents—all parents—and toward friends. But they also like to know that parents are there even though they might not actually like to be with them. If regular visits during the teenage years work out well, consider yourself lucky. But if a particular teen does resist going on visits, focus more on keeping a continuing relationship and don't worry or be overly offended if he or she prefers scheduling life the way he or she wants to.

ATTACHING STRINGS

Sometimes the not wanting to visit and other problems stem not so much from the child's initial attitude as from a parent's not so positive feelings about the visits—an ambivalence that the parent often communicates to the child.

"Bye, Mommy's darling. Have a good time at your father's. I'll be lonely without you, but don't you worry about Mommy. She's a big girl. And don't forget to call to let her know how you're doing. And what should you do while you're there?"

"Stay out of the cellar because it's too damp and might give me sinus headaches."

"And what else?"

"If I start getting a sinus headache, call you immediately."

"That's my very good boy."

"Bye, Mommy."

"Have a good time, Mommy's special pumpkin. Four o'clock Sunday it'll be all over and you'll be back with me. All safe and snuggly at home."

Getting the Message

As we've discussed, letting your child have a relationship with your ex is in your child's best interest. To encourage that relationship, sometimes you need to take care that you don't openly express your own misgivings.

WHEN KIDS SHUT OUT A PARENT

At first, after their mother and I split up, I saw Eva and Justin pretty regularly. But then within the first six months Eva started making excuses about not coming. About a year ago she refused to come on the visits altogether. I still see Justin regularly, but I really have no contact anymore with my daughter. Even when I call the house to speak to Justin or to their mother, if Eva answers she just says, "What do you want?" and then immediately gets Justin or her mother. I don't really understand any of it. Before the divorce I had a closer relationship with Eva than with her brother. I feel completely rejected.

"Why don't you want to see your father?"

"Well, he *is* a jerk. I never liked it when I did go with him. After all, it was *him* who left *us*. What's his problem?"

"But you used to like him."

"I was just a kid then [she's now thirteen]. I didn't understand what a jerk he was."

Kids may gradually move away from a parent for many reasons. The parent may have been genuinely difficult—overly critical or harsh. The parent may have constantly tried to involve the kids in parental battles with their other parent. Sometimes children are simply not comfortable with a parent whose personality style is very different. Regardless of why, sometimes kids will shut out a parent, and it's very hard on this parent.

One temptation is to assume that the ex is in some way behind it all—which may or may not be the case—and to go after him or her.

"Angela, I don't know what you're saying to Eva. But you know that she and I always had a good relationship before the divorce. It's not fair to me and it's not fair to Eva. What went on with the divorce was between you and me."

This invariably backfires. What's more, the rejecting child always gets to hear about it, further bolstering his or her case against the offending parent.

"Dad thinks I don't like him because Mom wants me to think that. He is such an asshole. The reason I don't want anything to do with him has nothing to do with Mom, it's because he *is* an asshole. I don't know when he's going to get that through his thick head."

It only makes matters worse, often producing another and sometimes more permanent alienation. So what can a parent do? The best thing to do is to play it very straight. If the aim is to have the relationship resume someday, you need to take the position: *I love you and I'm here.*

If your kids won't talk to you, send a note.

"I know you don't want to see me. But I want you to know that I love you. And whenever you want, I would like to see you again."

You should send birthday and holiday cards and presents, though not elaborate ones. In effect, keep saying, "I'm still here."

Your children still may reject you and your cards or presents.

"What an idiot. He still sends me stupid birthday cards and presents. All I do is throw them away."

However, that is far better than

"See, he doesn't even care about me. He didn't even send me a birthday card."

There is also no question that this rejection, even though usually temporary, can be one of hardest and most embittering consequences of a divorce. Yet most of the time patience and persistence win out. The relationship resumes and often ends up being quite good.

"I'm not really sure what my problem was with Dad. What I can remember is how angry I was at him. How much I hated him. But I'm a little vague about why, though I remember being mad at him for hurting Mom. But he always kept in touch, though I thought he was an idiot for doing it. But then I started seeing him again, just a little bit at first. And then it got to be like we had a relationship again. Like nothing ever happened. I see him regularly now. It's no big deal. We're friends."

SWITCHING HOMES IN ADOLESCENCE

"Hello, Edward, you are going to have to come over here right now and pick up your daughter."

"But it's one-thirty in the morning."

"I want her out of this house. Now. And I want her out for good. I don't care what you do with her. She's yours. I have had it with her. I mean it."

Or the just as frequent other version of the same story:

"Hello, Dad. You have to come and pick me up."

"But it's one-thirty in the morning."

"I can't stay here in this house one more minute. Mom is crazy. I can't live here. I can't. You have to come get me."

Once kids of divorce reach adolescence, a *very* common phenomenon is that at some point they switch homes. And sometimes they switch back. And sometimes they switch back again.

There can be many reasons for all the moving, but the most common is that they are teenagers. With adolescence comes the inevitable conflict: Your child has one view of what he or she wants to do with his or her life, and you have another.

"I want to do well in school, which she doesn't believe. I'm not a drug addict. If she would just get off my back I could have a life. I'm allowed to have fun. You only get to be a teenager once."

If I could trust her, I would get off her back. But I know I can't. She thinks she knows everything. But she doesn't. She's just a kid.

With the advent of adolescence, the difference between what they want and what we want for them becomes more serious because the stakes go up: drugs, drinking, and sex are all now very real parts of their lives. But also with adolescence comes a normal, healthy urge to be more independent. This part of the adolescent makeup feels that a parent's very existence is an insult. It makes them feel childish. As a result, many adolescents temporarily seem to develop an allergy to their parents, especially to the one to whom they feel the closest. The result is that normal day-to-day parental interventions—

"Angie, pick up your room."
"Bruce, don't you have any homework?"
"Tracy, I want you in at eleven-thirty, no later."

—can regularly turn into major conflagrations:

"I can't come in at eleven-thirty. You're crazy. I'm not going to let you ruin my life. I'm not a baby like you think I am. What the hell gives you the right to tell me what to do? You took drugs in high school. You're so full of shit when you boss me around."
"Diana, don't you dare talk to me that way. I'm really getting fed up with you."
"Well I'm already fed up with you. I hate living in this fucking house with your stupid fucking rules."

During these firestorms, it's not unusual that another home, another parent, can become a very attractive alternative. And the switch often occurs.

"Why did you have to get a divorce?"

She thinks that she is going to get away with everything at her father's. That she's going to be able to do whatever she wants. I'm just being a parent, but she thinks the grass will be greener over there.

As long as the other parent is willing to have the child live with him or her, if your teenager wants to make the switch, there usually is not too much you can do about it. Courts vary greatly in how they handle issues of child custody, but for the most part, if a teenager wants to change homes, the courts will do nothing to stop them unless there has been substantiated abuse in the home to which they want to move.

Sometimes such switches end up being to the detriment of a given teen. The new home truly provides no support and the child flounders. However, more often than not, switches aren't so bad. But they don't eliminate all the problems either. If there were parent-child conflicts in the previous home, there are probably going to be the same conflicts in the new home. After all, there still are rules to obey, there still are curfews, there still is homework to be done, and there still are dirty clothes that have to be picked up.

"Mom was a lunatic. But Dad can be a real jerk too. They just don't understand what it is to be a teenager."

Occasionally teenagers gain some insight and begin to see that what they believed was a problem caused by a lunatic parent had more to do with a basic problem of their own: they are stuck still being a kid, not yet old enough to be able to live on their own, and in no way fully in control of their own destiny. They get to see that the world will change only so much and that they must learn to live with what they have, not what they want. As a result of this new understanding, the demon parent gets less demonized.

However, the one big benefit that can come with switching homes—and perhaps one of the few parenting advantages that can come with being divorced—is that the new home can temporarily defuse a volatile situation. Some parent and teen battles can truly get out of control and take on a life of their own. Both parent and child get pulled into ongoing struggles and both end up as losers. Switching to the other parent's home can be a safe way to "run away" from such overwhelming conflicts.

When kids choose to switch homes in their teenage years it feels like a rejection, a condemnation of you as a parent, or at least a strong statement of preference for the other parent. Yet usually it's simply a decision they've made because they're teenagers and to them the grass looks greener at their other parent's place. But usually they find out it's not as green as it looked.

CANCELLATIONS AND NO-SHOWS

Kids often make problems about seeing another parent, but the reverse can also be the case. The kids may want to go, but the parent cancels or simply does not show.

It breaks my heart to watch it. Danielle and Brenda so look forward to the times with their father, and then he calls at the last minute with some sort of excuse. Or sometimes he just never shows up. And they both get so disappointed.

There's little that you can or should do to protect kids from the disappointments dealt out by their other parent. Intervention by you brings, at best, temporary changes, but it can never hold off the disappointments produced by a neglectful parent. The kids do get disappointed. It can be hard to watch. And it can be hard to deal with the fallout. But if the unreliability of a child's parent is part of a regular pattern, it's something they will have to learn to live with. This is who they have for their other parent: someone who's unreliable. And in time, especially if you stay out of it, they will adjust.

"Why did you have to get a divorce?"

"Dad says he's going to take me this weekend. I hope he does, but I know I really can't count on it. It's what I always say about Dad no matter what he says: maybe he will, but maybe he won't. Brenda calls him Maybe Dad."

Or sometimes they end up taking a more negative view.

"Dad's such a jerk. I don't care if I go with him or not. If he really cared about me he wouldn't have stood me up all those times."

That is, they harden. But if they're going to be regularly disappointed, they must.

As with other problems the other parent causes, you don't want to come to his or her defense.

"You know how your father gets to be very busy."
"Yeah, watching football on TV."

The fastest and best adjustments come where the reality of a situation is clear and not in any way disguised. Even unhappy realities.

"Dad's a jerk. I can't believe anything he promises."

To which the wise parent says nothing. Danielle is exactly right.

Unreliable Ex's—What to Do

It's ridiculous. Their mother is completely unreliable. I can't count on anything with her. She doesn't show up. She's late. She brings them back late. She brings them back early. She'll totally screw up my plans and thinks nothing about it. It's not fair. I'm reliable. But because she's so unreliable, I'm stuck being the one who has to do everything at her convenience. She gets away with everything and I'm the one who's inconvenienced. It's completely unfair. I had plans yesterday to go out and then she calls up at the last minute and canceled and I had to cancel my plans. It drives me crazy.

Often the other parent's unreliability is a problem not just for your child, but for you as well. There's no question it's unfair, two adults having to work together, one acting like an adult, the other more like a child.

I get after him. I've done everything I can think of, but nothing I do or say ever really changes anything. That's the way he was with me. Why should I expect he would be different now that we're divorced?

But unreliability can be handled rather simply if you plan accordingly.

"You're going to pick up the kids at six, right? Is six okay?"
"Yeah, six is fine."
"I need you to be there at six because Lindsay [his girlfriend] and I have plans and we need to leave the house by then."
"Yeah. Don't worry. I'll be there. Don't have a cow."

For starters, always build in extra time. Say six but plan on six-thirty. If your ex comes on time, fine. Second, *never* make important plans that depend on an unreliable ex doing what he or she says he or she will do. That leaves you far too vulnerable to being hurt, upset, and mad. In short, don't count on an unreliable ex suddenly becoming reliable.

I cannot believe she did this to me. I had a job interview—which she knew. She was supposed to be there at nine-thirty and I had to

Waiting for Dad

be out of the house by ten, and she shows up at ten forty-five. She said her laundry took much more time than she thought it would. I can't believe her. I actually missed the job interview.

If you have something important like a job interview that you absolutely must get to by a certain time, don't count on your ex. Even if it's inconvenient, make other plans. Don't depend on someone you know is unreliable. This is where a support network of relatives and friends—if you have that luxury—can be valuable.

If the other parent's unreliability creates problems, you have a right to be tough. You have a right to set a time limit, making sure the other parent knows about it. At the specified time—leave.

"Denise, we're going to the movies with or without the kids. We will be leaving the house at six-thirty p.m. If you get to the house to pick them up before then, fine. If not, we'll take the kids to the movies with us."

But it's still not fair that I have to be the adult, and she gets to do what she pleases.

That's right, it's not fair, but this issue can be evened out. The unreliable ex forfeits any right to make demands about the "when and where" of visits. You get to call all the shots. You get the right to dictate the time and place according to what's convenient for you.

"Hey, Eileen, I thought I'd come over tomorrow night and take out the kids."

"Mm, let me think about it. . . . No, I don't think that will be so good, Ed. Wednesday night is too tight with my schedule. But if you want to, Thursday night would be fine."

"Ugh, I can't do Thursday night. I've got softball."

"Well, you let me know any other time when you want to see them. Wednesdays really are my only bad nights, so any other night really is fine."

"Yeah, well, I'll call."

10

If You Are the Other Parent

SECOND-CLASS PARENTHOOD

"Ralphie."

"Oh, hi, Dad. Mom wants to talk to you."

"Oh, I'm glad you called, Neal. Lynn Ellen has been sick and she says she's not feeling well enough to go with you this weekend."

"Can I speak to her?"

"Of course, Neal."

"Lynn Ellen, your mom says you don't want to come this weekend."

"Gosh, Dad, I was out of school today. I threw up this morning. Maybe I really should just rest this weekend."

"You could rest at my house."

"I know that, Dad. But I really don't feel good. I'm still feeling sick. Would you really mind? Here, I'll let you talk to Mom."

Lynn Ellen's mother comes to the phone.

"Neal, I think Lynn Ellen's embarrassed. She doesn't want to hurt your feelings. But she really has been pretty sick and you know how when she's sick she just likes to be here."

"Oh, okay. Let me talk to Ralphie."

"RALPHIE! Your father wants to talk to you. . . . What? . . . Ralphie says his program has started but he'll see you tomorrow night. Five-thirty? Right?"

"Yeah, I always come at five-thirty."

"Ralphie will be ready. Bye, Neal."

Sometimes I really don't see the point of it. I've always done my part. I arrange my life around being able to have time with the kids. Sometimes we have a good time when I'm with them. But sometimes I think they're bored, especially Lynn Ellen, and they wish they could be back at their mother's. I love them, but sometimes I feel I could be doing other things with my time rather than entertaining them, and that they would like that better too.

I just don't feel I'm that big a part of their lives. Being with me is something they're supposed to do. I don't really know that much about what goes on with them day-to-day. I'm not there. It's like their mother controls everything. I really think they look upon me as some kind of second-class parent. Sometimes I feel like saying screw the whole bunch of them. I do.

Despite how it may seem from the standpoint of the parent who has the kids most of the time, being the noncustodial parent is not always fun and games. A lot of the day-to-day stuff, unpleasant as it sometimes can be, also breeds an intimacy that less frequent parenting can lack. The bottom line: many second parents end up feeling a lesser degree of connectedness to their children.

It's not that I don't love them. I do. But sometimes I feel that they're more of a responsibility than that I'm a part of their lives. I don't feel I completely know them. I certainly don't know them as well as their mother does. I just don't feel that I'm such a big deal to them.

And, of course, having a relationship with one's kids also means having a continuing relationship in some form with one's ex. Sometimes that's no problem. But often it is, and this injects an additional flat-out negative into the relationship with the children.

Seeing them and dealing with them means dealing with her. The divorce was supposed to end that. You would not believe how I cannot get through the slightest interaction with her about the kids without her carrying on about something, without her turning anything I say into something to bitch about. She is unbelievable.

The Importance of You

Yet despite how much effort maintaining a regular relationship with your children can be or how unrewarding it can sometimes seem, there are huge benefits for both parent and child. Underneath it all, children are *not* indifferent about their relationship with their less frequently seen parent. They care greatly, and they care intensely about that other parent.

"What do you think of your dad?"
"I like him. He's a good guy."
"When was the last time you saw him?"
"I don't know. Not that long ago. Maybe a year ago."
"When was the last time you talked to him?"
"I don't remember. I guess it was my birthday."
"When was that?"
"November."
"What month is this?"
"July."
"You haven't talked to your father in six months?"
"No, he's kind of busy."
"And you love your father, even though he hasn't even called you in the last six months?"

"Yeah. I told you."

"What kind of father is that who doesn't talk to his son for six months?"

Ricky suddenly starts to get teary and his face reddens.

"My dad loves me. It's not his fault. What the hell business is it of yours anyway?"

The desire and need to love and be loved by their other parent is so strong and desperate that kids will even build a fantasy around that parent if necessary. They will take an enormous amount of neglect and even abuse, and if there is the slightest chance for a little something good from that parent, they'll come back for more. They will reject a parent, hate a parent, but never quit caring about a parent. And in their hearts, they hold out hope that someday, somehow, their love and caring will be returned. As adults they can look back and see clearly whether a parent was there for them as children. If a parent was *never* there for them, they can acknowledge it and they mourn.

I wouldn't say I always liked my dad. I still think he was a jerk to Mom. And sometimes he was just a jerk. But he loved us. And he kept seeing us. And I know a lot of divorced dads didn't do that. I always knew I had two parents. I always knew if it ever really came down to it, he'd be there for me.

Looking at how they sometimes treat you, it is understandable how you as a noncustodial parent can wildly underestimate your own importance to your children.

The way they act toward me sometimes, the way they'll talk to me, like it doesn't matter what they say to me, I feel they take me for granted.

Which they often do with a parent they know they can count on—but if someone else were to ask them,

"Do you think your father is a good father?"

"Yeah."

"Why do you say that?"

"Because he is. He takes us with him. He's nice to us. I mean, he's not always nice to us, but you know what I mean. He's a good father."

"Do you love him?"

"Yeah. Of course."

"So if you think I'm a good dad, how come you and your sister can't be nicer to me? Why can't the two of you show me more respect?"

"Oh, hi, Dad. You heard all that stuff?"

"Yeah, so why can't you show me more appreciation some of the time?"

"I don't know. 'Cause you're my dad."

"What's that supposed to mean?"

"I don't know."

Now, your importance to teenagers can be especially hard to discern. Teenagers can do an excellent job of making each parent feel like an unwanted appendage. With adolescents, you have to take comfort in the long-range outlook. Teenagers may indeed seem to reject you and have zero interest in your active presence in their lives, but at the same time, they care that you are there for them. Especially looking back, teenagers know and care that you were available *if* they needed you.

FEELING POWERLESS

Sometimes I can see the kids talking just like her. They'll even use the same words she uses. I mean, I don't mind that, but she's not a good person—and I'm not just saying that because I don't like her —which I don't. But what she does with the kids, I can see what she's doing to them. I worry how they're going to grow up.

I only get to be with them for a little of the time. I watch them getting older in front of my eyes and I think about how she is with them. It scares me and there's nothing I can do about it.

But there is. What you can do is choose to spend as much time with them as possible. By spending time with them, you provide a very different experience of what it is like to be with a parent, an experience that will be as good and as positive as you can make it.

"Dad's *real* different than Mom. I don't think Mom approves of Dad at all. I don't tell her about Dad and us anymore because I can see how it always gets her upset. But I like it at Dad's. He's nice to us. He's very different than Mom."

Their alternative experience with you will become a part of them. In effect, a competing view of the world and a different way of relating to other people become a part of them. But your very powerful influence cannot become a part of them unless you have chosen to spend time with them and be a continuing, ongoing, consistent part of their childhood.

YOUR TIME WITH THEM—WHAT TO DO

Sometimes when I get Jackie and Caroline I don't know what to do with them. I don't know what girls like to do exactly. I'm always feeling that I have to do something to entertain them. They like movies, so we go to a lot of movies. Actually, I take them as much as I can, but I don't like always having to spend money on them. However, when we are back at the house, I don't know how to make conversation with them. I mean, I ask them about school and all, but beyond that I'm never sure what to say. It's fine when we go out, but back at the house, the truth is they end up watching a lot of TV because I don't know what else to do and they don't have any friends where I live.

Many noncustodial parents indeed end up being a form of Disney Dad, but not by choice. They can't figure out what else to do and feel that when they are with their kids, they always have to *do* something.

Yeah, I worry that if we don't do something fun, they won't have a good time. And if they don't have a good time, they won't want to come see me.

It is an understandable concern, and of course the kids don't help the situation, because they always are ready to be entertained.

"Please, Dad, please. Can't we go to Wonder Fun World? We haven't gone there in a month and it's so much fun. I'll love you forever if we can go. I will. And Mom never takes us there."

It's hard not to feel pressure to always be doing fun stuff during your limited time with the kids. However, doing lots of fun stuff is fun for kids, but it has little to do with what makes a relationship.

"Dad's great, but I don't know if I actually ever want to live with him. I mean, I don't know, I don't know if I'd feel really comfortable. But he's great doing all the stuff with."

If you are a noncustodial parent who sees your kids on a regular basis, the best plan of how to spend time with your kids doesn't have to include totally kid-centered activities. Yes, it is nice sometimes to do fun stuff, to plan activities that you know your kids will like. But much of the time can simply be spent going about your business, doing what you normally would do but with the one difference: They're with you. Taking your kids along on errands on Saturdays, having them in the kitchen with you while you chop carrots or sort laundry, or even just sitting next to them and watching TV together are all good things to do with your children. Maybe not as much fun for them as movies and arcade games, but they'll have much more interaction with you. These "nothing times" can have a lot in them.

"Do you want to try cutting the onions?"

"No, they make me cry."

"They make me cry too, but I splash my eyes with cold water and it stops."

"Daddy is a crybaby. Onions make him cry. Do you cry at sad movies?"

"Sometimes."

"I don't. I never cry at movies. But I did throw up once. Do you remember?"

"Yeah. We had to go home."

"Yeah, but we got the video."

But what if they get bored? What if they don't like the time they spend with me?

Sometimes they will be bored. Sometimes they will be bratty. Sometimes you won't get along, which is just like it is with any normal parent who spends any amount of time with his or her kids.

The secret of being a successful noncustodial parent is in building a separate life with them. If you hang in there, have regular contact, and become a part of their lives, your relationship will take on its own flavor, usually very different from what goes on when they're in the home of their other parent. Different because you are a different person and your relationship with them is, will be, and should be different.

Noncustodial Mothers

"Tanya and Inez don't live with you?"

"No, but I see them Wednesday nights and every other weekend."

"Oh. How did this come about?"

"Actually, at first they lived with me. But it really wasn't working
out, and both Ted and I felt that it would be better if they lived
with him. And it does seem better this way. For all of us."

"Oh. I see. WAITER. CHECK, PLEASE."

A prejudice that still hangs on is that there is something unnat-
ural about a mother whose children do not live with her—that
mothers whose children live with their father, not them, should
walk with their heads down and not meet other people's eyes.

The truth is, of course, that all kinds of circumstances dictate
this decision, sometimes of one's choosing—

"I really do like it much better this way. Ted really is a much
more nurturing type, has much more patience than I ever had."

Sometimes not—

"My company transferred me out of state, and I couldn't find
another job in the area. And the divorce decree said that I couldn't
leave the state and take the kids."

Being a noncustodial mother is a case where the problem really
is in the perception. What actually goes on day-to-day, whether as
noncustodial mother or noncustodial father, usually works perfectly
well for both the kids and the noncustodial parent. My experience
has been that for the great majority of families, those roles have
seemed quite comfortable for all—but with the same problems as
when fathers are in the noncustodial role. Very definitely a noncustodial mother is *not* less of a mother to her children.

But it is also true it is a lesser role. And there will be times, as we've seen, when a noncustodial mother may feel like a secondary parent. And it is hard for a mother not to feel a little defensive.

Kids who live in such circumstances do not see it as strange at all. *They* have no trouble with it.

"Why don't you live with your mother?"

"I don't know. That's what they decided."

"Don't you feel it's a little strange? Most kids live either with their mother or with both parents."

"No. I live with my dad most of the time and I get to see my mom."

To them it is just the way it is.

The perception problem is not in the kids' eyes. It's in how the adult world thinks.

I'm not really that surprised. There always was something a little odd about her in high school.

But the bottom line is that to the extent you can free yourself from worrying about the perception of others, being a noncustodial *mother* simply will not be a problem.

11

Bringing In New People

Sooner or later, if it hasn't happened already, you or your ex may get a new partner—for companionship, for sex, maybe for marriage. And you can be sure that your kids will react. The introduction of a new partner for a parent always stirs up all kinds of feelings in children—some of which may definitely be negative.

New Partners—Soon After the Separation

Kids are in a state of shock after first hearing about a separation or divorce. They're worried about what's going to happen and wishing they're having a bad dream that will go away and return their world to the way it was. Their world has been picked up and shaken, with pieces flying all over the place. Gradually, but *only* gradually, they will, like a tuning fork that has been twanged, stop shaking and begin to assess the new world around them and get used to it.

They're getting a divorce. I can't believe it. They're getting a divorce.

Since it takes a while for the shock to recede, shortly after the divorce is *not* a good time to introduce anyone into a new role in their lives.

"Richie and Janice, you remember Mr. Henderson. Well, Mr. Henderson and I are more than just friends."

They're getting a divorce. I can't believe it. They're getting a divorce. And Mommy has a boyfriend. I can't believe it. They're getting a divorce and Mommy has a new boyfriend. I can't believe it.

It's just too much too soon. Give them a chance to adjust to the big news of the divorce—first. If that means holding off on seeing more of someone you're very interested in, then that's what it means. If you have been and want to continue seeing someone without the kids' knowledge, that's your business. But bringing in the news of a new partner at the same time as the divorce is asking too much of them. It's too overwhelming. It's simply not fair to them.

In a few situations, kids will have no problem with the immediate introduction of a parent's new partner, especially where a child feels that the divorce, although shocking, is nevertheless a good thing.

"Daddy used to hit me and Mommy. I'm glad he's gone. I want Mommy to have a new nice husband who maybe will be nice to me and who doesn't hit her and doesn't always make her cry."

In other situations—most situations—when is it okay to deliver the news of the new partner? Not weeks, but months. Two months? Three months? Six months? It's hard to know. There's no set answer because you can't know how your children will react. And you have to read how they're getting over the shock of the divorce. You have to let them begin to get used to *one* new life before you introduce yet another.

But if there is another person who is a significant part of your life and it is clear that that relationship is going to continue, you do not want to hold off too long on what is a reality in both your life and your children's lives.

"Bernice, can we talk?"

"Sure, Mom."

"You remember when you were growing up, and after your dad left, how I never let you in my bedroom after nine p.m.?"

"Yeah?"

"And how I had a separate outside entrance to the bedroom built?"

"Yeah?"

"And how you always asked me about voices in there, which I always said was just the TV?"

"Yeah?"

"Well, dear, I want you to meet your stepfather, Leonard. We've been married for twenty-two years now."

"Hi, Leonard."

"Hi, Bernice. Nice to meet you. Your mother's told me a lot about you."

YOUR EX'S PARTNER—WHEN IT'S TOO SOON

Monday he moves out of the house into an apartment and that weekend he has the kids over and she's there. I can't believe he could be so insensitive to the kids. How dare he have her over there when the kids just found out about the separation four days ago? They're still in a state of shock and now they have to deal with her too? I understand his right to see the kids. But with her there it's like he's forcing her on the kids. When I think about her with the kids I feel that they are somehow being violated, that something is being forced on them that they are in no way ready for. And they have no choice about it.

It's poor judgment on the part of your ex, but you can't do much in a situation like this. You have very little control—none, really—over who's with your ex when he sees your kids. You can express your concern, but this probably won't do much good. If you resort to lawyers and courts, a judge might agree that immediately after a separation is too soon for a new partner to be brought into the kids' lives, but this judge is rarely going to forbid the presence of the new partner when your ex is with the kids. (This would only happen where there's a question of abuse on the part of the new partner.)

This situation can be hard on the kids, and it can also be hard on you. You're still getting used to the idea of the separation and now you have to deal with this other person as well. Regardless of who initiated the divorce or how you currently feel about your ex, it's hard not to have—at least initially—strong negative feelings about any new partner, especially if that new person pops up immediately.

However, in the long run, it's perhaps not quite as bad as it may seem. There's no question that it *is* tougher on the kids to have to deal with this new person right away. But if your ex is going to have a new partner, sooner or later that person will become part of your kids' lives whether or not you or they like it. It's just that it would have been better if it had been later rather than sooner.

WHEN YOUR KIDS DON'T LIKE YOU TO DATE

"But, Mom, I don't want you to go out. I'm going to miss you. I'm going to be scared. It's not fair to leave me alone."

"You're not going to be alone, Jessica. You know Marjorie [a teenage girl who lives next door] is going to be here with you."

"But I don't like Marjorie. I want to be with you."

And Jessica bursts into tears.

Kids often don't like you to date. They don't like the idea of sharing you with anybody else. Sometimes they will do all they can to make dating difficult.

"Why did you have to get a divorce?"

"Please, Mommy, please, please don't go out. I'm gonna be so lonely, please. Just this time. Please, Mommy, please."

But how do I know that she doesn't truly need me, that my going out won't really hurt her?

Good question. Following the breakup of a marriage, children can need their parents to be there *just for them* even more than before the breakup. However, divorce can make children more clingy, and clinginess is not always a sign that a child *needs* more of you, only that he *wants* more of you. Want and need are not always the same.

Do You Spend Enough Time with Your Kids?

How do you know if you are spending enough time with your kids, that by dating you're not violating some deep need of theirs? As Jessica demonstrates, kids are keenly aware that other people in your life take away from your time with them, but, unfortunately, they're not an especially reliable barometer in regard to this question.

"Jessica, tell me honestly. Do you think I spend enough time with you?"
"No, I get sad. I get lonely. I miss you."

Maybe she does, but maybe she doesn't. Maybe Jessica is just saying that because she thinks her answer can get more of you.

So how *can* you know? If you are out *constantly*—whether dating, working, or exercising on the cross-trainer at the health club —then you're probably not spending enough time with your children. If you're not there in the afternoons because you work, not there most evenings because of various commitments, and then not there on weekends, if you don't see them because they go to visit their other parent—then you're probably not spending enough time with them. Or if your busy schedule is compounded by their Scout meetings, soccer games, and piano lessons, and you feel you rarely see them other than "Hello" and "Goodbye," you probably don't spend enough time with them.

However, if you regularly spend time with your kids, if they know they can count on you for significant chunks of time when it is just you and they, then they're probably getting enough. This is true even if much of that time is daily routine activities—chauffeuring them around town, cooking and eating, getting them to clean up, getting them ready for bed, plus some time—it doesn't have to be that much—that has no purpose. Still, if you're unsure about whether you spend enough time with your kids, spend more—if you can.

GUARANTEED TIME WITH YOU

"I used to have lots of time where it was just me and Dad. But then he started seeing Emily, and then they got married. And now I don't have any time where it's just him and me. Emily's always there. I don't feel anymore I can tell Dad stuff like I used to, especially if it's about things that I don't like between Emily and me."

With the presence of a new partner, children can easily feel that they're being shut out. An important rule that goes a long way toward keeping your kids from feeling resentful toward your new partner is to make sure that they still have special access to *just you*. It is very important for them to know that they can always have time with you if they want. It doesn't have to be very frequent, nor does it have to be very long. But they *must* be able to count on it.

"I know I can talk to Dad if Emily pisses me off. Which she does a lot. Dad doesn't actually do much about it, but at least he listens."

"Why did you have to get a divorce?"

If it is true that your children can always get private time with you, then you can know that you have gone a long way toward avoiding one of the biggest problems that can come with having a new partner as part of your and your children's lives. By keeping in place the special relationship between you and your children, you can know that regardless of what happens with a partner who may come into your lives, what matters most to your children has been preserved.

Who Controls Whom

If you're certain you're giving your children adequate time, spending time with a new partner can often be more about the issue of who controls whom. The key point is that it needs to be you, not they, who control the giving of your time. If you think they need more of you, then fine, give them more. But it shouldn't be your kids who decide where, when, and with whom you spend your time. You don't want them to dictate the dispensing of your attention. Be sympathetic—but only to a point.

"I know you don't like it when I go out."
"But you can't go out. I don't feel good. I don't want you to go out. I hate that new babysitter."
"I'm sorry you don't feel good. I'll come in to kiss you when I get home."
"No, please don't go. Please. You can't. Don't go."

But at that point this is exactly what Jessica's mother should do.

Some younger kids—rarely teenagers—don't even like to share you when you're at home.

Whenever Carl comes over, Jeffrey always butts in. He simply will not let Carl and me talk. He'll actually stand between us and talk about the dumbest stuff and make it impossible for us to have a conversation.

If they're alone with you, they can be happy for long stretches with no attention from you at all. They can tolerate your inattention because they know that *should* they want you, you would be immediately available. Bring in a new partner and their piggiest nonsharing urges take over. Perhaps they were never good about sharing you, even when their other parent was in the home. But whether they are long-standing parent-hoggers or newly extra-clingy ones, they see this new person getting special attention from you, and it drives them crazy.

"Mom, Mom, Mom, don't you and me have fun when we play Monopoly? Mom, remember how I got hotels last time? Can we do it again? Can we? Mom, Mom."

What you do not want to do is to drop everything and attend to them.

"I'm sorry, Carl. I know you and I had wanted to spend the evening together, but Jeffrey wants me to play Monopoly with him, which usually takes us about three hours. So I guess you'll have to go home unless you want to watch us play Monopoly."

Here firm does best.

"No, Jeffrey, I'm talking to Carl. If you can't be here without always interrupting, then you can't stay here in the room with us."

If he persists, send him out of the room. The issue here has nothing to do with Jeffrey's not getting enough of his mother and one hundred percent to do with his wanting to be in control of his mother. Again, giving your child this kind of control is not something you want to go along with.

For Some Kids Sharing You with a
Potential New Partner Can Be Difficult

How Kids Look at New Partners

Obviously, kids can have a full range of feelings toward a new partner—anywhere from enthusiastic acceptance to hostile rejection. Which reaction you will get depends on the nature of your children, their ages, and what your new partner is like. However, certain issues concerning new partners usually inspire negative feelings in most kids, regardless of their age or situation.

For example, the introduction of a new partner has one very

definite meaning. For kids as well as for their parents, the presence of a new partner signals that the old marital relationship really is over. Now "they" will never get back together again.

"I don't know. I know it's stupid, but I had always hoped that maybe Mommy and Daddy would get back together. But now that Mommy's with Freddie I guess it's never going to happen."

Not only can new partners signify the true and final end of their parents' marriage, but also kids often feel that the new partners are intruders into the *old* family. Even if the old family unit was split up by the divorce, at least the *members* of the family remained the same.

"Freddie's not part of our family. I don't want anybody new. I want it to be still our family—just me and Caroline and Mom. I don't want Freddie. I don't want anything more to be different."

The new partner not only is an outsider but is also being injected right into the middle of their family—and not by their choice.

"If Mom wants to have a boyfriend, I suppose that's her right. But I don't see why he has to be part of my life."

Of course, the issue of loyalty often arises with the introduction of a new partner. Many children—sometimes assisted by a parent —feel that liking the new partner would be betraying their other parent.

"If I like Rosa, does that mean I'm being disloyal to Mom? Wouldn't it hurt Mom's feelings if she knew I liked Rosa?"

As time goes by and kids get used to the fact of the divorce, they may look at the coming of a new partner differently. They may have accepted their parents' separation as a fact of life and may not even mind the new addition.

"Well, since I know Mom and Dad are never getting back together, I actually wouldn't mind having a guy around the house if he was nice to me, and Mom liked him."

NEW PARTNERS AND YOUNGER KIDS

The truth is that much of your kids' reaction to a new partner depends on how old they are. In general, the younger your kids, the more accepting and welcoming they will be to a new partner.

Kevin's mother to her six-year-old son:

"Kevin, I want you to meet Philip."
"Hi, Philip. My name's Kevin. Do you want to see my hamster?"

Kevin's mother to her fifteen-year-old son:
"Kevin, I want you to meet Philip."
"Mumble."

Ten months later.
Kevin's mother to her six-year-old son:
"Kevin, how would you like it if Philip came to live here?"
"All the time?"
"Yes."
"That would be good, Mom. I like Philip. He's nice. Do you think he would play with me a lot?"

Kevin's mother to her fifteen-year-old son:
"Kevin, how would you like it if Philip came to live here?"
"But, Mom, he's an asshole."
"Don't say that, Kevin. Besides, Philip likes you. And I'm sure you will get to like him once he lives here."

"No, I won't. He *is* an asshole. I don't know how you can like him."

More often than not, those two stories really portray the way it would be if the only difference were the kids' ages. Younger kids, because of their age, because of their level of emotional development, will typically have quite different reactions to a new partner than will older children, especially teenagers. And the difference is that younger kids (up to the age of maybe nine or ten), even if they have an ongoing relationship with a second parent, are typically open to making caring attachments to new caring, friendly adults who come into their lives. They look upon all adults, until proved otherwise, as potential sources of nurturing. They don't have any conflicts with liking and perhaps coming to love a parent's new partner.

"But if you like William, don't you feel that it's not fair to your father?"
"I don't know."
"What do you mean, you don't know?"
"I like William and I like Daddy."

Sometimes younger children will have some concern about divided loyalty, but even so, it usually won't conflict with their feelings toward the new parent partner.

"I like William a lot. But maybe that hurts Daddy's feelings. I still love Daddy best. But I like William a lot too."

However, like older children, they are susceptible when the other parent makes loyalty a problem.

"William was over there again when you were at your mother's, wasn't he? She certainly can't stand being alone, can she?"

But even then, though younger kids will feel the pull of loyalty, when they are away from the disapproving parent, they'll like the new person nonetheless. They just learn to keep quiet about it.

> "I know Dad doesn't like William. But I do."
> "Do you ever tell your dad that you like William?"
> "No."
> "Why not?"
> "Because I know it makes him mad. I don't usually say anything when Dad asks me about William."

If partners turn into stepparents, younger children can still handle the situation rather easily. Having two same-sex parents living in different places—two fathers, as it were—doesn't pose any special problems for them.

> "Don't you get confused about having two fathers?"
> "No."

They simply are not confused. To them their two "fathers" are two different people with whom they have two different relationships. Whether they call one Dad and the other William, or call both Dad, they know that one is their natural father and the other their stepfather.

> "There's Dad, and there's William, but I call him Dad too. I always know who I'm talking about."

In fact, where a stepparent comes into the life of a child quite early—before the age of two or three—they take on full-parent status, from the child's point of view. If a stepparent comes in early, grows to love a child, and stays in the home through the rest of his or her childhood, he or she becomes a parent to that child—even if the child has a same-sex biological parent whom the child has been seeing all along. From the child's standpoint, both are parents.

"But which is your *real* father?"
"They're both my real fathers. One's one father and the other is the other father. Two fathers. Daddy Jim is my biological father and Daddy Clark is my stepfather. Get it?"

We might be confused by it, but they are not. Both men are fathers.

NEW PARTNERS AND OLDER CHILDREN

Teenagers will treat a new partner or a stepparent the way they treat all adults or even worse. But a teenager's dislike for a new partner has little to do with who the partner is. It has mainly to do with being a teenager. Most teenagers are aggravated by their own parents' presence.

"Does Mom have to be in the same room as me? Doesn't she understand how aggravating she is? The way she breathes, and that look she always has."

This same negativity can get directed at a new partner, untempered by the loyalty that teenagers feel toward a natural parent.

"Who is he? Why should I care something about him? What do I owe him?"

Also, with adolescence comes puberty and with puberty comes a whole new issue that definitely can go against any potential partner of their parent. Teenagers begin to experience and understand sexuality and have enough trouble dealing with their own. The idea of their parents having sexual feelings is totally unacceptable,

Age Is a Factor in Children's Receptivity
to a New Partner

and the idea that a parent would actually seek out a sex partner is
a thoroughly revolting concept.

"My mom actually has sex with William. That's disgusting. She
never did with Dad, except of course the two times when they
made me and Brenda. And maybe once on their wedding night.
But I know they never liked it. Mom's disgusting and William's
disgusting. They're both disgusting."

The result is that a teenager often acts toward his parent's new partner in a way that is far from nice. More often than not this behavior has little to do with anything specific that the new partner does or does not do wrong. More usually it simply comes because your child is a teenager.

WHEN YOUR KIDS AND YOUR NEW PARTNER DON'T GET ALONG

Sometimes the match between your kids and a new partner may not be good. Maybe your kids don't like your partner.

"Mom, why does Bruno think he's so smart? He's so bossy. You know, I don't think he likes kids at all. All he does is yell at us. I don't even think he likes us being in the same room with him."

And maybe your partner doesn't like your kids.

"I'm not saying it's your fault, but those kids are spoiled, Helena. And Keith's voice. It just sets me on edge. He's always so loud. Doesn't he have a volume control?"

It is not necessary that kids like your new partner or that your partner like them. People can live together with little fondness for each other. If your relationship with your kids remains good, then their relationship with your partner is definitely of lesser importance.

However, this enmity must not translate into constant conflict, because that can be a significant problem.

"Mom, Bruno's yelling at me again."
"Goddamnit, Helena, can't you teach that little brat to stay out of drawers he's been told not to go into."

Certainly you want to give the relationships time to improve. Sometimes professional counselors can help, but, unfortunately, sometimes the conflicts don't resolve themselves. Then you are faced with a very tough choice. Will having this new person as a permanent part of your life create a home that is filled with too much ongoing friction and tension? Will the continuing conflict end up being too unpleasant for you, too unpleasant for your kids, and in the end maybe also destroy the relationship between you and your partner?

If your kids are teenagers and may soon be moving on, the decision is easier. You can wait a little while and then become a permanent couple. But if the kids are younger, and your home is filled with intense conflict and tension and will be for many years to come, maybe the best choice is to end the relationship. Sometimes the sad fact can be that your right to adult love and companionship may turn out to be incompatible with your wish and duty to provide a loving home for your children.

Changing Partners as Losses for Your Kids

I really liked Bob, but then Mom broke up with him and I was real sad. But then Jim moved in and I really liked Jim. But then Mom and him broke up too, and I was real sad. Now Bill lives here. And I don't like him too much. So I hope Mom and him break up pretty soon. But I still miss Bob and Jim.

Younger kids, especially, will often make very real attachments to new partners who become part of their lives. If a relationship ends, it is a loss for your kids. If there are multiple partners, it can mean multiple losses.

"Mommy, please don't make Bruce leave. I don't want him to go. If Bruce leaves I'll miss him so much."

But Bruce did leave and eight-year-old Jeanine, who had grown to love him, went into a real slump for the next couple of months.

I mean, I knew that would happen. But it was not working out with Bruce and me at all. I was not going to keep him around for Jeanine's sake. But when he left it really did hit her hard.

Kids can become casualties in adult love relationships. Should you avoid possible relationships with new partners because of possible future losses for your kids? No. But you do need to be aware—and to weigh as part of your decision—that any long-term commitments, should they not work out, will mean losses not just for you but quite possibly for your kids as well.

Taking a Long-Term Partner

Ricky and Rosie were four and six, respectively, when their parents separated. Two years later the divorce was final. For five years, the kids mainly have lived with their mother, Lydia, but have seen their father, Alec, regularly. They've gotten used to these arrangements and rarely think back to the time when their parents lived together. Ricky and Rosie are basically content with their lives.

Following the marital breakup Lydia dated some. But a year ago she met Ned, whom she likes a lot. And now she and Ned want to get married. Ned would move in and live at the house that had been Lydia's since the days of her marriage to Alec.

Lydia has given it a lot of thought. She loves Ned. He's different from Alec. She thinks Ned is nicer, more stable. She thinks that a relationship with him would work. Lydia wants more than just occasional nights over and some evenings together. She wants to live with him. She wants to share her life with Ned. And Ned seems to want this too.

The kids like Ned. They frequently do things together, and Ned comes over to the house regularly. But Lydia is unsure about how

Ricky and Rosie will react to the prospect of her marrying Ned and his moving in as her husband.

"What do you think, kids?" she asks them one evening.

"Does that mean he'll live here all the time?" asks Ricky.

"That means he'll sleep here every night, doesn't it?" pipes in Rosie, taking on a look of displeasure. (Ned has already slept over occasionally.)

"Yes, he'll live here. We'll be married."

"And he'll be our stepfather?" asks Rosie.

"Yes."

"I don't like it," says Ricky. "Can't you just keep dating? I don't want him to live here. I like it the way it is. Just us."

"Yeah, I don't like it either. I don't need a stepfather. I already have Dad. It's okay if you date. But we don't want you to get married." And Rosie starts to cry. "If you want to marry Ned, wait until Ricky graduates from high school. Then you can do whatever you want."

"Yeah, wait until I graduate from high school," echoes Ricky.

But Lydia doesn't want to put it off. She doesn't want to wait nine years to marry Ned. She doesn't know how Ned would react but doubts that he'd be interested in waiting that long. Besides, she wants him to move in *now*. She wants to marry Ned.

"Why? What's the problem?" Lydia asks her children.

"This is our house," answers Ricky. "You and us. It will be different if you and Ned are married and he lives here all the time. If he lives here, then it's his house too, and then he can boss me around. It won't be just my house and our house anymore. It will change everything. I like it the way it is—I don't want you to marry Ned."

But they'll see. Once Ned moves in it won't be like they think. It will work out. Ned's a nice man. They'll like having him live here and being more a part of their lives.

196

And maybe Lydia is right. Maybe if she and Ned were to marry it would work out well for her, Ned, and the kids. Despite what the kids think. Maybe they would adjust well, just as Lydia hopes. Maybe a few years down the line, were we to ask the kids how they feel, the new marriage will have been a success for everybody.

"What do you think, Rosie?"
"Now that they're married and Ned's been living here, I think Mom's happier. And I know she's been nicer to us. It's okay having Ned as a stepdad."
"How about you, Ricky?"
"I like having Ned around. He's funny. And he's not bossy like I was afraid he was going to be."

But you never know what's going to happen. Sometimes it doesn't work out. Many children of divorce, now looking back as adults, will tell you quite clearly that the advent in the home of a parent's new partner was a turning point in their own lives—for the worse.

"Once Dad married Leslie everything changed. She was the boss in the house and Dad wouldn't stand up to her. I had had a real nice relationship with him before he married Leslie. But after that, it was like I lost him. I didn't even like being around the house anymore."

YOUR NEEDS AND THEIRS

Bringing a new partner into your children's lives has a big impact on them. Often this can be to the good. The new partner enriches your life and your children's as well. But the main reason parents seek out new partners has nothing to do with the best interest of their kids. It has to do with their own wants and needs. It has to do with their quest for happiness in their own lives.

"Why did you have to get a divorce?"

Should I date? How soon? Should I see somebody whom the kids don't like? Should I have somebody move in? Should I remarry?

Only you can be the final judge of what is fair to you and what is fair to your kids—how you can reconcile their needs with yours. But whatever you decide to do, it *will* have an effect on your children and you need to give careful thought to what your decision will mean to them. In the end, whatever you decide, you must be able to live with it. These are not easy choices. But nobody ever said they would be.

12

Parenting with a New Partner

Ryan, his mother, Suzanne, and her fiancé, Gary, are in the family room watching TV. The program they're watching has just ended.

"Well, that's it, Ryan. End of TV for tonight," says Gary.
"Mom!"
"Gary, I usually let him stay up to watch *Nobody's Home*."
"Suzanne, you let him wrap you around his little finger. Ryan, you've already watched enough TV. Suzanne, he doesn't need to watch all that crap."
"MOM!"

Who should be the boss in a home that includes the parent, the child, and the parent's partner?
Who's the boss of what and when?

"He's not my father. He can't tell me what to do. What gives him the right to boss me around?"

"Why did you have to get a divorce?"

"I'm going to be his stepfather. I already live here. I'm already part of the family. I have to have rights too about what goes on. Besides that, I watch the way Ryan manipulates his mother. And Suzanne just doesn't see it. What I'm doing is for his own good."

I can't believe Gary and Ryan. It's like they're both kids. I feel that no matter what I do I can't win.

How this issue gets resolved can often determine whether the new relationship works out or not. As with any new living arrangement, everyone wants to stake out precious turf. And with the addition of a new partner into a previously set home life, each person is understandably very wary about what he or she may gain or lose. The feelings involved can be very strong indeed, and regarding who has the ultimate authority, your children have a valid concern.

He really isn't my dad. He doesn't love me as much as Mom does. I can't count on him in the same way as I do with Mom. We haven't had a life together. Why am I supposed to trust him to be the boss of me as much as my mom? He can't just walk in and suddenly boss me around. What gives him the right?

A new partner, even with the status of full stepparent, is not their parent in the same way that you are. There is not the history together, there is not the commitment, and above all there is not the love. What this boils down to is that, overall, your new partner should not have the same "boss" status as you. You are your child's full parent; your new partner is not.

PRESERVING YOUR CHILD'S SPECIAL STATUS WITH YOU

The first step in preserving your full-parent status with your children is to make it clear that your kids will not lose their special relationship with you. When you bring a new partner into your life (and often a new partner's family members), you want to make certain that your kids know that you'll always be their main parent in the home.

Before Gary came, I always knew that Mom loved me more than anything, that I was special to her. I knew that if I wanted something that she didn't want to give me I could plead real hard and sometimes she would give in, just because she loves me so much and doesn't want to disappoint me. Sometimes I used that to take advantage of her. Sometimes I even felt a little guilty. But I always knew I had this special place in her heart.

But then Gary came. And now I feel like he's trying to take that away from me. When she lets him decide about what's going to happen with me, I feel like she's deserting me and like I'm losing the special stuff I had with her. It almost feels like I'm in a foster family, like I'm losing my mom.

Our love for them gives them special privilege; they can play on our strong feelings. They possess a card that says they are special, and that assures special treatment from us, different from anybody else's—except a sibling's, who they begrudgingly understand gets a special card too. It's the difference between having a parent and having a caretaker.

My dad loves me more than anything, and that gives me special power with him. Gina [the father's new wife] is nice and all, but I don't have that special "she loves me above everybody else" deal that I have with Dad.

That special status is desperately important to kids and to us. That special status is our love for them, which becomes a part of them and is the first and most important piece of what makes them feel good about themselves. It's the very best that parents have to give to their kids, and they treasure it.

Therefore, in a household that includes you, your kids, and your new partner, any set of rules that's going to work must recognize one basic right of your children.

Because I am the children's true parent, I must be the one who has the final say about anything that has to do with them.

Rules for You, Your Kids, and Your Partner

What follows is a list of rules that keep within the framework of the above requirement—that you are the ultimate boss of your kids. Your partner has rights too, and these are recognized within the rules that follow. These rules can eliminate much of the worst day-to-day conflict that inevitably arises among you, your kids, and a new partner.

When it's just your partner and your child, your partner is the boss. For example, when your partner and your child are both at home and you are not, or if they go somewhere together and you do not go along, your partner is in charge. This is the same rule that you have when you put your child in the temporary care of any adult—for example, a babysitter or a teacher at school.

"Deena, don't play there with those cars. You'll scratch the floor. Play on the rug."

If they disobey, your partner will probably tell you.

"While you were gone, all Deena did was give me a hard time."

If your child complains to you, support your partner.

"Deena, when it's just Brian and you, he is the boss."
"But, Mom, you always let me play with my cars on the floor and I never scratch anything. Why do I have to listen to him?"

"When it is just Brian and you, you have to listen to him. He's in charge."

The rule backs the authority of your partner when he or she is alone with your kids. It also says to your children that in those situations they are on their own. However, if what occurs goes against the way you want it to be for your child, then you can later intervene with your partner.

"Dad, yesterday after school, Elisa said I couldn't go outside unless I wore my green winter jacket. But you know it's so bulky. I can't play anything in it. I can't do anything in it."

Let's say that Carey's father agrees with her that it's okay for her to play outside in a lighter coat. He should intervene.

"You know you have to do what Elisa says, but I'll talk to her about your wearing a different coat when you go outside to play."

And later to Elisa:

"Elisa, I know it's been cold lately, but I think it's okay for Carey to go outside in a lighter coat. Her green coat really is no good for playing. I think she'll be warm enough."

This doesn't challenge your partner's right at that time to insist on the heavier coat. But it says what is to happen in the *future* and it states the larger principle that regarding general rules for your kids, you are the one who sets the overall policy, you are the boss.

A frequent tactic when kids are left alone with a stepparent and they don't like what's going on is to call their natural parent.

"Dad, Gloria won't let me have any Crackly Peanut Bars."

Although her father usually lets her eat them, at this point he shouldn't intervene. He should not get Gloria on the phone and say:

"Hi, Gloria, it's me. Trish says you won't let her have any Crackly Peanut Bars. But it's okay with me if she does."

He should wait until Trish is not around to talk to Gloria.

"Gloria, it's okay for Trish to have a couple of Crackly Peanut Bars in the afternoon."

Here, Trish's father is not challenging his partner's decision at that time. Rather he is asserting that he's the final authority on overall policy with his child.

But if they do call, do not even listen.

"Dad, Gloria won't let me have any Crackly Peanut Bars."
"That's between Gloria and you."
"But, Dad . . ."
"Is there anything else you want to talk about?"
"But, Dad . . ."

It simply does not work to be the phone arbiter. In practice it merely undermines your partner and drags you into situations you can well do without.

"That little brat. Anytime I tell her anything, she's on the phone to you."

When you and your partner are together with the kids, if your partner gives an order, back it up whether you agree with it or not. Do not contradict your partner in front of your kids. That undermines your partner's status and shows disrespect, and he or she will justifiably feel resentment toward you and your children.

Barry to Andrew, his stepson:

"No, Andrew [who tends to be overweight], you don't need a second helping of the mashed potatoes, you've already had enough."
"Mom, I'm allowed to have more potatoes if I want."
"Barry, let him have more potatoes. It's okay."

It doesn't work and it undermines.

"She makes me look like a fool in front of the kids. No wonder they treat me like I'm some kind of second-class citizen."

Better, because it doesn't undermine your partner:

"No, I'm sorry, Andrew, but no more potatoes."
"But, Mom, you never said I couldn't."
"Tonight you've had enough."
"But, Mom!"

If you disagree with what your partner did, later, but only later, you should say to him or her that you disagree with what was said, then state what you want the rule to be in the future.

"Barry, I know Andrew's overweight. But he's going to have to learn to discipline himself. If he wants more at supper, I don't want us to say no."

Again, it backs your partner at the time but gives the message to both partner and child that on policy issues you are the boss.

Also, when it is both you and your partner together, the general rule is that it is you, not your partner, who should give the orders to your kids. This rule is not ironclad. But the kids are your responsibility, and generally your partner should defer to you. He or she does have the right to disagree with you about your rules for the kids, but you must be the one who ultimately decides, even though you may run into strong feelings from your partner.

Over time, if your kids see that your partner defers to you, they will know that you have stood up for their right to have you as the final boss. This has a tremendous impact on your children and is a great reassurance.

Sometimes what you do with the kids has a direct effect on you and your partner's relationship, or directly on your partner.

"You let them stay up so late, when do we get time to be alone together?"

"Whenever you and I are talking, Lana always butts in. She feels she has to be part of every conversation. It's getting to be like we can't even talk."

"You're going to have to do something about Anthony and my tools. He keeps using them without my permission and he's already ruined a couple of expensive ones."

Where your kids' behavior directly affects your partner, you may have to modify what you've been doing. Your partner is now a part of the household and has rights too.

"But, Mom, that's not fair. Just because Jerry lives here, now we have to go to bed earlier. That's not fair."

But here there may be changes that they will just have to accept.

"No, I'm sorry. You can be in your rooms, but no more TV downstairs after nine."

"Mom, it's not fair."

Generally, for questions about the parenting of your kids, you must be the final judge. Maybe you do give in too much. Maybe you are spoiling them. Maybe you're not even a very good or skilled parent. But they're your children, not your partner's.

If you make clear to your partner:

"When it's just you and the kids, you're in charge and I will always back you up, and I will never undermine you in front of the kids. But overall I am the one who makes the decisions about my children"—

Your partner may not like it.

"How they behave affects my life too. I have to live with them. I really think that you're not tough enough with them. You let them get away with too much."

"I am sorry you don't like the way I'm raising my kids. Maybe I am wrong. If they grow up all wrong, I accept that it will have been my fault. But this is how I choose to raise them."

If in the end you stand firm on the position that you are the ultimate boss of your kids—right or wrong—rare will be the partner who will not, albeit grudgingly, concede that right. For they *are* your kids. And again, if you stand firm, it's unlikely that your partner will let that stand in the way of your relationship.

Everyone benefits from the rules because they make matters clear. If you screw up with your kids, then it's your fault. Which is fine, because you'd rather have it that way.

"Why did you have to get a divorce?"

If there are going to be mistakes in the raising of my children, I want those to be my mistakes.

HOUSE RULES

Some rules, though they pertain to your kids, affect everybody—in effect, house rules. These include rules about shared living areas, cleaning up, rules regarding how much noise can be made and when it can be made, rules about things that must be shared, like the video game system. Such house rules need to be the same for everybody.

"Michael, I know you don't care, but I don't like your kids putting their feet up on the couch with their shoes on."

Or:

"Grace, I know it doesn't bother you, but it really does bother me when Denise and JoJo play their music so loud."

When behavior affects joint space, house rules should apply. And with house rules, your partner should have equal say. You are the one who ultimately sets the rules for your kids, but with house rules, you and your partner have to work it out between you—as do all adult couples.

WHEN YOUR KIDS ARE DISRESPECTFUL TO YOUR PARTNER

Kids, especially teenagers, can be amazingly nasty to new partners.
"Hi, Curtis."
Curtis walks right by.
"I said hi, Curtis."
"What?"
"Is it asking too much for you at least to say hello?"

"Are you going to do this every time I have to go through a room that you're in?"

"All I was asking was that you might recognize that I exist when I greet you."

"Bill, you married Mom, but you didn't marry me. I don't have to do anything."

Curtis exits.

You actually have some control over situations like this. The rule is that if the disrespect goes on in front of you, don't let it pass.

Another conversation between Bill and Curtis, but with Curtis's mother present:

"Curtis, how did your soccer game go yesterday?"

"What? Is this supposed to be the 'Good Interested Stepfather' performance?"

"Curtis, you know that I don't want you talking to Bill that way."

"Why? What does it have to do with you?"

"You heard me, Curtis. I want you to show Bill normal respect."

"Why? I don't respect him."

"You heard what I said."

When Curtis's mother steps in, his show of disrespect to Bill becomes a matter between Curtis and his mother. She makes it clear that he is answerable to her for this disrespectful behavior just as he is for any other bad behavior.

"Regardless of how you feel about him, I want you to treat him with respect."

This has power—despite what your kids might say.

If the nasty behavior goes on when you're not there, you may get to hear about it from your partner.

"Rene, this afternoon before you got home, Samantha was getting herself a soda out of the refrigerator and I nicely asked her if she would bring me one and she says, 'No, you can get your own. You're so lazy.' I really had asked her nicely."

These conflicts can be like sibling squabbles, but there's a major difference. Your partner is an adult and must be treated as one by your kids. If your partner complains about similar situations, you must always bring it up with your child.

"You may not like Bill, but I expect you to treat him in a civil manner."
"I don't see that I have to. I didn't marry him."
"No matter how you feel about him, I want you to treat Bill with respect."

Although you may not always agree with your partner, your kids see that you nonetheless will back your partner's right to be given the full respect adults deserve. They also get to see in yet another situation that in regard to rules for their lives, you, not your partner, are the boss.

Rules with Long-Term Partners

If a partner has been there for a long time, and he or she and the kids have gone through a lot of life together, and if during that time the partner has shown consistent caring and commitment to your kids, we're talking about an entirely different situation. Especially when this partner has been in the home since the child was very young, children will look on this partner as a *true* parent, which is really what he or she is. That's what a parent is: someone who over the long haul shows consistent caring and commitment.

"I love Derek. I think he loves me like Mommy does. I know I can always count on him just like I can with Mommy."

Because the kids see such partners as full-fledged parents, they should have full parental status, which means that they can be boss of the kids too and the kids *will* accept that status. With a longtime partner, kids do not say,

"You're not my dad."

Because they really feel that he is.

MIXED FAMILIES

A prominent part of the contemporary landscape is the wide variety of different and complex family situations, situations that include not just new parent partners, but new siblings as well.

"At Dad's, it's Laura [his wife] and her two kids, Tinker and Glenn, except that they're only there half the time when we're there because the times we visit Dad is sometimes the weekends that Tinker and Glenn are with their dad. At Mom's house, it's Mom and Leo [her boyfriend] and Tracy. She's sixteen. She's Leo's daughter who has lived with us full-time since last March because she and her mother fought all the time. Vinnie and Lindsay [Leo's children by another marriage] come most weekends."

In my experience, this kind of arrangement isn't such a far-out example. Who lives with whom, where and when, for how long, can get pretty complicated and frequently changes.

Is all this complexity and change regarding who is "family" and where and what is "home" disconcerting and problematic for kids? It can be, yet the reality is that what kids look to as the foundation of their security, as discussed repeatedly in this book, is the continuing major presence in their life of at least one loving parent. This above all else.

But clearly, with all the change and the complex family arrangements, with the introduction not just of new adults in the home but new children as well, problems do arise.

"Okay, kids, now everybody sit down together. Now that we will all be living in the same house these are going to be the rules. Charlie and Kevin, because Rusty and Renee have had an eight-thirty bedtime when they were living at the apartment with Jim, and Jim says that he wants to stay with that as their bedtime, your bedtime is now going to be changed from nine-thirty to eight-thirty. You kids of course understand this, because if you still stayed up to nine-thirty that wouldn't be fair to Rusty and Renee since they are the same age as you two. Also, there will be no more eating dessert in the TV room since Rusty and Renee have always had to finish their meals at the table, and Jim wants it to stay like that. I know this is a change you may not like, but I also know that both of you understand that it has to be this way now that we are all going to be living together."

"Sure, Mom," perks up Charlie, "we gotta all pull together now that we're gonna be part of the same family."

"Yeah," chimes in Kevin, "if we don't have family harmony, what do we have? Everybody has to sacrifice something. I don't mind."

Not exactly.

"Mom, are you crazy? No way. This wasn't our deal. You get to have a live-in boyfriend and me and Kevin get to go to bed earlier? No way. We didn't ask to have Jim here."

One of the toughest problems with new siblings in the home is that families with two different sets of rules and customs—including house rules—are now supposed to live together.

"It's not fair. Denise goes to other kids' houses after school and I have to come right home every day."

Anthony E. Wolf

How does one reconcile the ongoing conflicts between fairness and the changes that are demanded of children who had no part in bringing about those changes? Fortunately, there are certain approaches that can help you steer your way through these very treacherous waters.

Probably the most important step is recognizing and acknowledging that Charlie and Kevin's basic argument is valid. They're being asked to give up what had been the normal way of their life and accept a deal that is neither for their benefit nor of their choosing. Charlie and Kevin are the clear losers. Not only is their complaint valid, but their loss is a potential source of deep resentment which, if left unresolved, will continue as an unending source of friction within the new family.

"Dad, Charlie won't give me a turn on Death Star 300. You said we were supposed to share."

"Charlie, you know we got the game for everybody to share."

"Rusty, you're such a baby. You always run to your dad."

And later:

"Mom, I hate Rusty. I don't want to share anything with him. If it weren't for him here, I wouldn't have to go to bed at stupid baby times."

When two separate families are joined, the changes for any individual child need to be kept to a minimum. In this case, Charlie and Kevin keep their own bedtimes. If at some point Charlie and Kevin's mother wants to switch their bedtime to an earlier one, she can. But if she does, the decision must be clearly hers rather than a reflection of what Jim wants. Furthermore, if she changes their bedtime, she had better be ready for Kevin and Charlie to give her a particularly hard time about it, because they will.

But what about Rusty and Renee, who certainly will see the later bedtime of their new housemates and definitely won't be happy?

"Why did you have to get a divorce?"

"But it's not fair," screams Rusty when told he has to go to bed at his regular eight-thirty time. "Charlie gets to stay up until nine-thirty and I'm a whole month older than him."

There is a simple answer to this.

"No, your bedtime stays at eight-thirty."
"But it's not fair. How come they get to stay up later?"

The best answer is also the true answer, which kids do recognize in their hearts:

"Because I am your parent and that is my rule. Charlie and Kevin's mother has her own rules."
"But it's not fair. It's not."

They will persist. But if Jim does not pick up on their argument and stays firm—

"No, your bedtime is eight-thirty"—

Rusty will back off. He will realize that in this case this particular argument—"It's not fair!"—will not sway his father to change the bedtime. He also comes to look at the bedtime disparity as he would were it a friend his age who had a later bedtime: he's envious but also aware that the reason for the difference is that that kid has a different parent.

"You sure are lucky, David. Your parents let you stay up till nine-thirty. I wish my dad did, but he's a real jerk about bedtime. He treats me like I'm two."

Yes, it rankles, but not a whole lot. For the bottom line is that in this home the children have different parents. The two adults are not jointly in charge. As it was before they all lived together, Rusty and Renee's father makes the rules for them, and Charlie and Kevin's mother sets their rules. They may fuss, especially if they think their fussing can gain them some leverage, but they also will accept that the rules that affect them individually—bedtime, watching TV, doing homework—may be separate and probably not equal.

When entire families mix, the issue of house rules—rules to be followed by everybody—can be more complicated.

"Dad."

"What is it, Ginger?"

"Nancy's a lunatic."

"What are you talking about? You know I don't like you talking that way about her."

"But she is. She's after us about every littlest thing. I do pick up. But if I put something down for a second, she starts yelling. You should have just heard her. She was yelling at me about my school jacket. Yeah, it was on the floor, but I just took it off and I was going to hang it up."

"Well, you should have hung up your jacket."

"But it's not just that. It's everything. When it was just us, you didn't care. You didn't get after us about stuff at all like she does. I can't be a neat freak like Randall or Denise [Nancy's children who live with them]. You didn't raise me that way. She's ruining my life."

Obviously, the house rules that each family brought with them from before can be quite different. As with couples and roommates, neatness can often be an issue. Let's say that before Ginger's father married Nancy, he ran a household that was much more lax about picking up. Then Nancy, who had been much more strict with her kids about neatness, moves in and starts making the same kinds of demands on Ginger. Is that fair to Ginger? As with Kevin and

Charlie in the earlier story, it was not her choice that her father remarry.

"No, it's not fair. I shouldn't have to pick up so much. We got along fine when it was just us and Dad."

But here there is a difference. Yes, it is a change, a change that makes Ginger's life more unpleasant—she gets nagged more and has to pick up more. But the difference is that what is being asked is neither a torture nor something that Ginger shouldn't be doing anyway. To help her with the new house rule, her father can recognize the change and be sympathetic:

"I know it's different with Nancy here. I know I was much more of a slob about things than she is. And I know that you're not used to having to pick up more."
"So I don't see why I should have to do it. It's not fair to me."

But very definitely sympathize only to a point.

"I know you don't feel it's fair, but Nancy lives here now too. And we all are going to have to learn to be neater."
"But it's not fair."
"No, maybe not. But I expect you to pick up better."

And if, as often happens, Nancy is the one who is doing most of the enforcing of the house rule—

"I don't see why it should always have to be me getting after Ginger about picking up. You're her father. You should do more of it"—

She has a good point. Ginger's father *should* take more active responsibility in getting his daughter to meet unaccustomed neatness standards.

"Ginger, please don't leave the towels in the hall."
"You're just saying that because of Nancy. You never cared before."
"Ginger, please pick up the towels."

Mixing families includes mixing personalities as well as combining living styles. An obvious problem is that new siblings do not always get along.

"Mom, I have to talk to you."
"What is it, Tina?"
"Mom, I don't mind Edgar, but I hate having Colin live here. He's always pestering me and he thinks he's funny, but really he's just gross. He comes in my room and farts and thinks it's a big joke. He doesn't let up no matter what I do. I hate it."

This is a tough issue. Obviously, you try to do what you can to make the relationship better, but some personalities are going to clash—and for as many different reasons as there are personalities.

"I hate Colin. I do. I wish he didn't live here. Why can't he live at his mother's? Probably because she couldn't stand him either."

Probably nothing will help the two of them get along, but you can at least be honest about the situation:

"Yes, I'm sorry that you have to put up with Colin. I know it was nicer for you before he was around."

What you do not want to say is something like

"I'm sorry, but you're just going to have to make the best of it. Sometimes life isn't always fair."

"Why did you have to get a divorce?"

True, of course, but also a fact that Tina is only too aware of. She doesn't need her mother to point it out. What she needs is at least some recognition that part of her life is now harder for her. She needs recognition from her mother that part of the new living arrangement *is* a bad deal for her. It doesn't change Colin, but at least it recognizes that Tina has a legitimate gripe.

"He can't maybe go live in a foster home? Mom? Please."

13

Parenting Today's Kids

HOW TODAY'S KIDS ARE DIFFERENT

"Jimmy, would you please take those glasses into the kitchen?"
"Yes." And Jimmy goes and does it.

How many kids today do that? Parenting today is underscored by a historical change that has taken place over the past couple of generations. That change has made most forms of harsh punishment that were once standard practice—beatings with a stick, hard smacks across the face—unacceptable practices that now fall into the category of child abuse.

Kids are well aware of this new standard, with the result that they no longer fear their parents as did children of previous generations, which is good. On the other hand, parents have lost a significant weapon from their parenting arsenal. Because kids don't fear their parents, they talk back more and in general obey less readily than kids of previous generations.

You hear all of the time,

"I never would have talked to my parents that way."

Parents today think they're doing something wrong, that they are failing as parents, if their kids talk back to them or don't immediately obey. They berate themselves for failing to meet a standard that is both of the past and a direct product of a child-raising practice they have rejected. But they are not failing as parents. Regardless of whether you are single or married, parenting kids today is not always easy. Although divorce complicates the picture, the job becomes easier even in the toughest situations if certain basic truths about parenting—what works and what does not work—are clearly understood.

Behavior with You, Behavior with Others

Obnoxious behavior on the part of your kids doesn't mean that there is something wrong with them or that they're going to be bad people as adults. The behavior that you get is neither the same way they act away from home nor a reliable indicator of how they'll act when they're grown-ups.

As I briefly mentioned earlier, each of us has a "baby self" that rules at home and a mature self that goes out and deals with the world. Parents invariably get the baby-self version from their kids. Just the presence of a parent brings it out in all its splendor.

"But why can't we go get candy on the way home? Why can't we? It's not fair. Why can't we? Why? Why?"

"I don't understand it. Jeremy was behaving so well until you showed up. He and Justin have been playing so well all afternoon. I don't understand it. He must be tired."

Jeremy may be tired, but that's not the reason he started to fuss. His behavior went to pieces because his father's presence automatically elicited Jeremy's baby self. Parents experience this phenomenon on a regular basis. Kids who are angels all day in day care or at school fall apart the minute their parent picks them up.

And remember the mother's frustration in the "Sunday night phenomenon," when her kids returned from a weekend visit with their dad:

What is their problem? Every time they go to visit their father it's the same thing. As soon as they get back they're horrible. And they stay horrible. Sometimes it isn't until they return from school on Monday that things finally get back to normal. Not that the two of them are perfect—they're not—but they're always much worse after visits to their father's.

On top of that, he always says that when they're with him, they're well-behaved, that they rarely fight. I've asked the kids and they say it's true.

You can see that the "Sunday night phenomenon" is part of a larger phenomenon. The type of behavior described by the mother is not reserved just for divorced parents.

Away from home, their mature selves take the stage.

"Your Susan is one of my best students. She's a real hard worker. And such a polite girl. You must be so proud of her."

"I'm Mrs. Anderson. You must have me confused with another Susan's parent."

"No, no, Susan Anderson. She's one of my stars."

But at home a totally different Susan.

"Susan, would you please help me carry the groceries inside."

"Why? That's not one of my jobs."

"Susan, would you please help me carry in the groceries? I need your help."

"But why? Why can't Tanya do it? She's just sitting on her butt all the time. You ask me to do stuff all the time because you just don't want to ask your precious Tanya."

What Doesn't Work with the Baby Self

"Jason, would you please take those dirty dishes out of the family room and into the kitchen?"

"But they're not mine."

"I don't care whose they are, Jason. I am asking you to take them into the kitchen."

"But they're not mine."

"Jason, will you please take the dishes into the kitchen."

"But you never ask Becky to do anything."

"Jason, you know that's not true."

"Yes, it is. You ask me to do everything and you never ask Becky to do anything."

"Jason, do you always have to put up a fuss whenever I ask you to do anything?"

"I'm not putting up a fuss. You always yell at me about everything."

"I don't always yell at you about everything."

"Yes, you do. You're yelling at me now. You always yell at me. And you never yell at Becky."

"Jason, I'm getting angry."

"See, you don't even like me. You hate me. You do. You only like Becky."

When going against the wants of your kids, you're usually going against the wants of their baby selves. The baby self will resort to any means to get what it wants and in that pursuit it will go on forever. Even if it doesn't get its way, it will gladly settle for prize number two: as passionate and as endless an amount of you as it can get. The baby self feeds on parent response. It will say anything and do anything just to keep you engaged. It has learned from experience what responses get to you and custom-tailors what it says to get the passionate response—or, from your point of view, to push your buttons.

Therefore, any action you take, anything you say past your initial intervention, will only work against you. No matter what tack you take, what strategy you try, *nothing* will work to shut up the baby self. Let's look at a few of these sure-to-fail strategies:

Lecturing:

"Shana, how many times do I have to tell you to pick up your toys when you're done playing with them? I am sick and tired of always having to tell you. You are going to have to learn. Do you understand?"

"But it's not fair. I do pick up. You just never see me do it. I do pick up. You always ask me when I'm in the middle of a program. I can't do it then. You always ask me at the wrong time."

Threatening:

"If you don't stop pestering your sister, forget about going skating tomorrow."

"But it's not fair. She started it. She called me a 'weenie.' Besides, I'm not pestering her."

Trying to make them understand:

"Justin, I know you like to bounce on the couch. But it can break the springs. And then we'd have to get new springs, which cost a lot of money. And we really can't afford that."

"But it won't break the springs. I bounced on it before and it didn't break the springs then."

Being reasonable:

When parents stopped using harsh punishment and decided to throw out intimidation as part of child raising, many of them thought,

Now that I'm being genuinely nice to my children, won't they be reasonable too when I have to disappoint them out of necessity and if I'm gentle and reasonable doing so?

Unfortunately, it doesn't exactly work out that way.

"Mom, can I have a Popsicle?"
"No, I'm sorry, Lisa. It's too close to supper. You know how if you eat too close to dinner it always spoils your appetite."

How many children then say,

"Gosh, Mom, you're right. It's true. A snack now would spoil my supper. Shucks, I guess I'll just have to go without a Popsicle."

What they say, of course, is:

"But, Mom, you'll see. This time will be different. This time it won't spoil my supper. It won't. I'm so hungry. I am. Please. Please."

And Lisa will continue arguing until her mother, fed up and angry, finally does end it.

"Lisa, get out of here. You are not getting a Popsicle."

But, as she leaves, Lisa still doesn't give up.

"You never let me have anything I want. You don't."
"Lisa, get out of here."

Or, a shorter but still common response to a parent trying to reason with a child:

"We've been all over this before. You're still getting over being sick, and I don't want you having a friend over, because it's too much running around."

"But that's not a good reason. That's a stupid reason. You have to give me a good reason."

Demanding:

Demanding that a child do or not do something enters into the most beloved of all baby-self activities, a battle of wills:

"Gretchen, do not throw the ball in the house."
"But why?"
"I said do not throw the ball in the house."
"But why?"
"You heard me."
"But why?"

The baby self will not give up in a battle of wills. If its first strategy doesn't work, it quickly tries another tactic:

"Mom, can I stay up an extra half hour to watch *Five's Too Many*? They have a special show on tonight that's all about kids my age. Can I stay up, please?"
"No, I'm sorry, Egan, not tonight."
"But, Mom, please. It's a really good show. It's educational."
"No, I'm sorry, Egan. It's time for bed."
"But, Mom, it's a special show. You don't understand. Just tonight. I won't ask again. I promise."
"No, Egan. It's time for bed."
"But, Mom. It's not fair. I never get to watch anything special."
"You know that's not true, Egan. There are times I've let you stay up later. But not tonight. I want you to get ready for bed."
"Yes, it is true. You never let me watch anything special. When was the last time? When? I *am* gonna watch it."

"Why did you have to get a divorce?"

"Egan, you better 'watch it' all right, or I'm going to start cutting your allowance."

"But it's not fair. It's not."

"Why can't you just do what I ask without always giving me such a hard time?"

"I'm not giving you a hard time. You're the one who's not letting me watch my show."

Or:

"But, Mom, it's not fair."

"I'm sorry you think so, Kyle, but no, we're not going to get you another gerbil."

"But you never let me have anything I want. My whole life is like that. I never get anything I want." And pathetic tears start trickling down.

"You know that's not true, Kyle," says his mother, a slight note of concern in her voice.

"Aha! A winner!" exclaims Kyle's baby self.

"Yes, it *is* true. Nothing ever goes my way." And the pathetic tears really start gushing.

Whatever will work. The baby self is infinitely cunning and totally shameless. As discussed above, its sole aim is getting its way, and if it can't, keeping the battle going with you forever, the more passionately the better, will do. It will never give up on its own.

YOUR BEST STRATEGY

If your aim is to get as little as possible of the obnoxious and unpleasant behavior that your kids readily dish out, you have one viable option: Say what you have to say, do what you have to do, and end. The less response their obnoxious behavior gets from you, the less that behavior will continue. The more you respond, the more you will get.

Anthony E. Wolf

"No, I'm sorry you can't have a Popsicle. It's too close to supper."

"Please. Please. Please. Just this time. Please."

"No, I'm sorry, Lisa."

"But, Mom, I'm so hungry. Please. Just this time."

"I'm sorry, Lisa."

"But you never give me anything special. Last week you got
Brendan that turtle. I don't get anything special and all I want is
a Popsicle."

But don't touch it. At this point, any more response will only
prolong Lisa's fussing.

"But why? Why not? Why?"

If Lisa keeps fussing to the point that being in the same room
with her is too unpleasant, she can be asked to leave, or you can
always leave. But Lisa's mother must refuse to keep the conflict
going from her end.

The big disasters of child raising arise when a child's continued
fussing finally wears a parent down and parents either change their
mind:

"You drive me crazy. Have a Popsicle. Have twenty Popsicles. I
don't care if you spoil your dinner."

Or they blow up:

"Lisa, I am sick and tired of your fussing. When are you ever
going to learn to take no for an answer? I am sick and tired of this.
Do you hear me? I am sick and tired of it. I am fed up. I am really
fed up with you. Do you hear me?"

In either case, the baby self hears you very well, and it's very
happy. The prolonged fussing, having achieved its goal, is certain
to be tried again whenever the baby self is not getting what it wants.

But the reverse is also true. If the baby self sees that its continued fussing or other obnoxious behavior is for naught, it will use it much less, although it won't give it up completely. However, most of the time the baby self will move on because it knows when a battle is being lost.

"I hate you. You're mean. You never let me do anything I want. It's not fair. Tisha gets to do everything and I never do. You always favor her. It's not fair. It's not."

If all that the baby self gets from you is nothing, the fussing will end of its own accord.

"What's for supper?"

But if I just ignore what they say, all the back talk, aren't I letting them get away with it? Aren't I giving them the message that it's okay? How will they ever learn to behave any better?

If you do not like their behavior, say so.

"Lisa, I do not like the way you are acting."

But say it once and no more.

"I'm not acting bad. You are."

Say no more at that moment. If you feel the need to say more, do so, but later, at a neutral time when the incident is long over.

"This afternoon when I said you couldn't have another Popsicle I did not like the way you kept fussing."

You need not say another word. They hear you loud and clear. Because of their deep love attachment to you, your words sink in.

Although they might not show it, they know they were wrong. Your words are their conscience and they can't keep them out.

Again, obnoxious behavior, talking back, and being uncooperative are not behaviors that in and of themselves are indications that your kids are inherently bad, or a sign of your failure as a parent. What these behaviors are is unpleasant. If you can make appropriate demands on your kids, avoid being regularly bullied into changing your mind or losing your temper, then you've done all you need to do in bringing up a child who will grow into a good, respectful adult.

CLASSIC BABY-SELF APPEARANCES

The baby self can make an appearance anytime, day or night. Here are a few classic versions of the baby self in common day-to-day situations, so that you can get a good sense of the full range of its behavior. Included as well are suggestions on the best way to deal with the baby self.

Out in public:

The baby self likes being out in public, where parents simply do not have as many options as when they're at home. Out in public some of the baby self's favorite tactics become especially attractive; for instance, tantrums.

Dexter and his mother are in the checkout line at the grocery store:

"I'm sorry, Dexter, no candy."
"But I want candy. I never get candy. I want it."
"No, Dexter, no candy."
"But I want it."
"No, Dexter."
"But I want it. I want candy."

"Why did you have to get a divorce?"

And Dexter then starts yelling, as loudly as he can, "I want candy. I want candy."

Making the scene all the more unpleasant for Dexter's mother are the other shoppers in line, now staring at her screaming child with disapproving looks.

What a little brat. Can't his mother do anything about him? People with children like that shouldn't be allowed out in public. What a disgrace.

In such situations, above all, you do not want to be bullied by the baby self. If it learns that tantrums in public are successful in getting its way, you will always get tantrums in public. The rule is simple: After your decision, you must stay with it and not respond to anything that the baby self then throws at you. What this means in public is that Dexter's mother must wait out the tantrum. She must continue on about her business, even if that means dragging along a screaming child.

This can be especially hard considering that everybody else who is watching wants Dexter's mother to do something, anything, to shut him up. But no, she should *not* yell, threaten, cajole, or give in—just in order to keep him quiet. Those tactics will only ensure that she will get more and bigger tantrums in the future. Always, what you want to give to a tantruming baby self is nothing.

Getting ready for school:

"Ollie, would you please get dressed. Your bus is going to be here in twenty minutes."

"But, Dad, I can't find my green shirt."

"Well, then get another shirt. There are lots in your drawer."

"But I want my green shirt."

"Ollie, will you please get dressed."

"But I can't find my green shirt. I picked it out last night and I can't find it."

"Well, where do you think you put it?"

"I don't know. I can't find it. You have to help me find it."

"Ollie, I really don't have time for this. You know I have to get myself ready and get out too. If you can't find the green shirt, wear another one. You have to hurry now."

"But I don't want to wear another one. I want my green shirt and I can't find it."

"Ollie, it doesn't matter what shirt you wear, you just have to get dressed or you'll be late."

"I don't care if I'm late. I don't want to wear another shirt."

"We'll find the green shirt this afternoon and you can wear it tomorrow."

"But I want to wear it today."

What the baby self likes to do in the morning is lie naked on its back and count dots on the ceiling. What it doesn't want to do is get dressed and go out. If pushed, it will only dig in its heels and happily get into fusses with you to whatever extent you are willing to oblige. In the morning, less is always better.

"Ollie you have twenty minutes until the bus comes."

"But I can't find my green shirt."

And unless Ollie's father knows exactly where the green shirt is or wants to engage in an active search for it, again the best response is no response.

"You have twenty minutes, Ollie."

"But I can't find my green shirt. I can't. I don't want to wear another shirt."

But again, no way does Ollie's father want to get into it. The best course is for him to continue to get himself ready.

"Why did you have to get a divorce?"

"But, Dad, I can't find my green shirt."

But if Ollie's father truly says nothing, goes about his business, Ollie's baby self is unable to engage his father in fussing and is forced to face the cruel reality—his bus *is* coming in twenty minutes. The vast majority of children do not want to miss the bus—despite what they might say as part of their fussing. And if Ollie's father stays out of it with only occasional time reminders—

"Ten minutes, Ollie"—

Though rushing and fussing at the end, Ollie gets himself ready, with no additional pushing from his father. The green-shirt issue magically resolves itself on its own. It was a one hundred percent baby-self issue to begin with.

"I hate school [which he doesn't]. I hate this shirt [a red one, which he doesn't hate]. Bye, Dad. I love you." And he runs out to meet the bus.

But woe to the parents—in reality, most of us—who try too hard to push their kids along in the morning. Anyone who does thereby falls into the baby self's fussing traps, and ends up only making the morning go backward rather than forward.

In the morning, less rather than more really works best. State the reality, "It's morning and time to get dressed and ready to go," and then give infrequent reminders—"You have fifteen minutes." Otherwise stay out of it.

Or bedtime:

Bedtime is a special dilemma for the baby self. Above all, what the baby self hates is being alone, separated from its parent. What bedtime requires is that a child not only be alone but be alone in the dark with only monsters and robbers for company.

"No, thank you," says the baby self.

Most parents define bedtime as that time when children are supposed to be in bed, lights out and quiet. But a more useful definition of bedtime is that time when all meaningful contact with a parent ends.

"Good night, Daphne. Good night, my darling. See you in the morning."

"One more hug?"

"One more hug."

"One more hug?"

"One more hug."

"Just one more hug?"

"One more hug, but this is the last."

"Just one more, please. Just one more to keep the monsters away."

If the usual routine is three one-more-hugs, then that one was the last, and the parent exits.

"Good night, my darling."

"Please. One more. Please."

But the parent has left.

Of course, the baby self does not give up that easily.

"Dad?"

"What is it, Daphne? I thought you were in bed."

"Can Grandma Nana who died see me in my room?"

"No, Daphne, go to bed."

"But I think I saw her eye watching me."

"No, dear, it was just your imagination."

"No, it wasn't my imagination. It was her eye and I could hear her breathing. I remember how she breathed."

"Daphne, you were one when she died. You can't possibly remember how she breathed."

"I do, and it was her and I can't sleep. I need you to be with me."

Remembering the definition of bedtime as the end of meaningful contact, Daphne's father should transform himself into a benevolent robot.

"Dad, can Grandma Nana who died see me in my room?"

"Go to bed, Daphne."

"But I saw her eye watching me and I heard her breathing."

"Go to bed, Daphne."

"But, Dad, I could hear her breathing. You have to come up to my room."

But the robot, which has replaced Daphne's father, has nothing more to say.

And if Daphne's baby self truly learns that bedtime means the end of any meaningful contact with her father, she will for the most part be truly resigned to the fact that once bedtime comes she is going to have to go it alone.

"Well, if it's not Grandma Nana, it probably is a robber. You're making me sleep in my room with a robber. I'm going to be awake all night, if he doesn't kill me first."

Sibling fighting:

"Mom, Carly pinched me."

"I did not. Christy is such a liar."

"I'm not a liar. If you don't stop it, I'm going to pinch *you*."

"Mom, Christy says she's going to pinch me."
"But, Mom, Carly started it. She said I have body odor."

We are taught that the wise parent quiets the two girls and then says,

"Okay, each of you. I want you to tell me—one at a time, no interrupting, please—just what happened."

Each daughter, knowing she will get her chance, then tells her side of the story. The wise parent, having listened patiently, then mediates between the two.

"It is not a question of who started it. Carly, you were wrong to pinch your sister. You should never hurt each other. But, Christy, you were wrong too in teasing Carly. I know it's hard, but both of you should try to think about what it feels like to be the other person and the next time you want to tease or pinch, maybe you won't."

"Gosh, Mommy, thank you," say both girls. "We will try our best."

Of course, such a resolution has not happened in all of human history—though there is one unsubstantiated report of such an instance in Davenport, Iowa, in 1972.

The reality is that, with siblings, saying, "Okay, each of you—one at a time—tell me what happened," in real-world language most closely approximates saying to a tankful of piranha, "It's feeding time and I'm the food."

With feuding siblings, you're invariably dealing with voracious baby selves who will always swiftly turn any argument between them into an endless case-pleading session with you. The absolute rule with sibling bickering is:

1. Do not intervene on one side or the other. Simply tell them to stop and separate them if necessary. Again, the exception is where you feel that one of them might potentially harm the other.

2. Do not listen to what went on.

They can work it out by themselves or they can't—in which case you intervene and separate them.

There is another added benefit if you hold strictly to these rules. You eliminate the number one cause of sibling rivalry: two siblings competing to get you on their side. If you truly never get into it, that huge source of sibling enmity is actually eliminated. Going back to the original dialogue:

"Mom, Carly pinched me."
"I did not. Christy is such a liar."

Absolutely the best response is:

"I do not want to hear about it."
"But, Mom, I have a red mark where she pinched me."
"I do not want to hear about it. If the two of you keep bickering, you're going to have to go into separate rooms."
"But that's not fair. Carly always starts it. She always teases me."
"You heard what I said."
"But, Mom."
And the truly wise parent says no more.

Jobs around the house:

Baby selves absolutely hate work, anything remotely associated with work, no matter how seemingly minimal the effort required.

Fifteen-year-old Danielle and her mother:

"Danielle, I need you to bring in about fifteen logs from the garage."

"But I can't."

"What do you mean, you can't?"

"I can't, I'm busy."

"Well, you don't look busy."

"But, Mom, I have to do my homework and I promised Ethan that I would call him about the party on Sunday."

"No, Danielle, I want the logs brought in now."

"But, Mom, you can't just expect me to drop whatever I'm doing because of something that you want done now. That's not fair."

"The logs need to be brought in."

"Well, I'll do them, I just can't do them now."

"Well, when will you bring in the logs?"

"Why are you harassing me? I will. Later."

For starters, to the baby self "later" means "never." If you want your children to do something that they don't feel like doing, the only time to have them do it is now. This also means that if they are legitimately in the middle of doing something else that you don't want to interrupt, wait until they are through to make your request. But if you want something done, you had better ask to have it done now.

"No, Danielle, I want you to do it now."

"But you're crazy. Why do you always tell me what to do? Why don't you make Edward bring in the logs? That's a boy's job anyway."

"Danielle, it's not a question of whether it's a boy's or a girl's job. I need you to bring in the logs."

"Well, I'm not going to, because you're being completely unreasonable." And Danielle storms off to her room.

The cold truth is that if you want your children to do something that they don't feel like doing, you must persist and, above all, not be lured into the countless traps that your child's baby self will throw at you in order to get you off the subject.

But doesn't that mean nagging them? And wouldn't nagging be feeding their baby self?

If you do not persist, they won't do it.

Mom hasn't said anything about me bringing in the logs. I guess she's given up.

The baby self likes not just parent contact but *emotional* contact. What it hates is an emotionless, robotlike, demanding presence—what I sometimes refer to as the "business parent"—cold, unflappable, and unrelenting.

"Danielle, I am still waiting for you to bring in the logs."
"Why the hell can't you leave me alone? I hate this house. I hate living here."
"Danielle, would you please bring in the logs."
"This is so stupid. The only reason I'm going to do it is to get you the hell off my back. It really is not fair."
"Thank you, Danielle."

Conclusion

"Mommy."

"Who are you?"

"I'm your daughter Cynthia, Mother."

"Oh, yes. I recognize you. You've changed your hair, haven't you?"

"No, Mother."

"Did you used to have a mustache? Were you the one with the mustache?"

"Mom, I want you to meet someone." And Cynthia wheeled her ninety-four-year-old mother to a sunny corner of the dayroom at the nursing home. Sitting quite straight on a chair was an elderly gentlemen.

"Mother, this is Edward."

"Hello, Edward. You look familiar. Did you change your hair?"

"Edward, this is Caroline."

The elderly gentleman grinned. "You're a looker," said the elderly gentleman.

"What?" said Cynthia's mother.

"You're a looker," repeated the elderly gentleman. "Anybody ever tell you you were a hot ticket?"

"No," tittered Cynthia's mother.

"Wanna get married?" said the elderly gentleman.

Cynthia's mother tittered again and blushed. "Well, sure," she said.

"Yesss!" said Cynthia.

And the second wedding of Cynthia's fifty-two-years-divorced parents was held two days later in the same dayroom.

"I knew it could happen. I knew it could happen," sobbed Cynthia.

They never give up. Somewhere—at least a little bit—always remains the dream of the idyllic childhood spent with two happy parents where the sun always shone and lemonade came out of water fountains.

Yet the bigger reality is about what actually goes on in their lives before, during, and after the divorce. What matters the most for children of divorced parents is what actually goes on in the rest of their lives. Which is where you come in.

Parenting today's kids is not easy. Neither is parenting kids who are going through or have been through their parents' divorce. But it can be done. Given the right ingredients of a childhood, divorce or not, your kids will have as good a chance as any to come out okay in the end. Divorce or not, success in parenting comes with your doing the best possible job that you can during the time that you are with your kids. You can do no more. But far more often than not, it will be enough.